The Horticultural Show Handbook

The Horticultural Show Handbook

The official RHS guide to organising, judging and competing in a show

For the guidance of organisers,
schedule-makers, exhibitors and judges

8th edition
Revised 2016

Royal Horticultural Society

Sharing the best in Gardening

Published by the Royal Horticultural Society:
RHS Media, Churchgate, New Road, Peterborough PE1 1TT, UK

Registered office:
Royal Horticultural Society, 80 Vincent Square, London SW1P 2PE, UK

Registered charity number:
222879 / SC038262

www.rhs.org.uk

© The Royal Horticultural Society
1953, 1956, 1972, 1981, 1990, 1999, 2008, 2016
First published 1953
Eighth edition 2016
ISBN 9781907057656

10 9 8 7 6 5 4 3 2

All rights reserved. No part of this book may be reproduced, stored in a retrieval system or transmitted in any form or by any means, electronic, mechanical, photocopying, recording or otherwise, without the prior permission of the copyright holder

Editor, RHS Specialist Publications: Mike Grant
Layout and typesetting: Jeremy Kirk
Cover design: Anthony Masi
Index: Oliver Ellingham
Editor, RHS Media: Chris Young

Photographs: RHS

Printed and bound in the UK by Page Bros, Norwich

Further copies of this book are available at RHS Gardens and from RHS Mail Order 01483 211320 www.rhsshop.co.uk

Contents

Preface	7
Publisher's acknowledgements	8
Getting Started	11
Organising a Show	17
Writing a Show Schedule	27
Suggestions to Exhibitors	41
Suggestions to Judges	53
Rules	59
Judging Fruits	63
Judging Vegetables	89
Judging Flowers and Ornamental Plants	129
Judging Gardens and Allotments	173
Judging Hanging Baskets and Outdoor Containers	181
Glossary	185
Index	197

Show stationery

Show stationery is available exclusively to societies that are affiliated to the RHS.

For information on prices and ordering visit the Support and Resources section of the RHS website at **www.rhs.org.uk/affiliatedsocieties** (click on *Support and resources* then click on *Stationery* under *Information pack*) or email **mailorder@rhs.org.uk**

Join the RHS Affiliated Societies scheme

All gardening clubs and horticultural societies with an annual membership subscription are eligible to join the RHS Affiliated Societies scheme. Your club or society should have a remit to promote horticulture at a local level. A package of benefits is available to all members.

For further information visit **www.rhs.org.uk/affiliatedsocieties** or email **affiliated@rhs.org.uk**

Preface to the 2016 (8th) edition

The first edition of *The Horticultural Show Handbook*, published in 1953, was an important landmark in the process of establishing and rationalising rules and regulations governing the exhibition of flowers, fruits and vegetables at horticultural shows. The guidance offered in the 1953 edition and subsequently updated in 1956, 1972, 1981, 1990, 1999 and 2008, has been widely accepted by organisers of horticultural shows, exhibitors and judges throughout the UK. This small book has become the standard reference for all those who organise or take part in events at every level.

The 2016 edition has been updated and simplified in consultation with specialist plant societies, RHS committees and other experts.

Some sections have been rewritten (notably Bonsai, Gladioli and Orchids) and all sections have been reviewed and minor amendments made. The most noteworthy amendments are that blueberries are no longer to be shown on strigs; that the recommended number of specimens for a dish of vegetables is now the same for collection classes as it is for single dish classes; that pompon dahlias can now be up to 55mm in diameter; and that large pompon dahlias are now included, in line with National Dahlia Society rules. Judging criteria for floating flowers, tomatoes shown as a truss, and advice on mixed classes and trug/basket classes have been introduced. A draft show schedule has also been included.

The experts involved have at all times tried to make the book as easy to understand as possible, hoping to encourage those new to showing. With this publication, the RHS hopes to inspire keen gardeners of all ages and levels of experience to enjoy and continue the tradition of exhibiting at horticultural shows.

January 2016

Publisher's acknowledgements

The publisher would like to thank the many people who have contributed to this revised edition, in particular Colin Spires who generously gave his time and expertise in chairing the working groups that undertook this latest revision. Members of the working groups who gave freely of their time and experience to dissect, reassemble and check the text to ensure its accuracy were: David Allison, Jim Arbury, Richard Bailey, Harry Baker, Peter Dawson, Gerald Edwards, Malcolm Evans, Malcolm Hill, Ivor Mace, Barry Newman, David Thornton and Medwyn Williams. All of the above would like to express their thanks to RHS staff Georgina Barter, Mike Grant, Jeremy Kirk and Chris Young, and freelancers Anita Foy and Louise Jackson who coordinated the revisions.

Thanks are also due to the numerous plant societies, show judges and individuals who provided advice on sections applicable to their own discipline: John Anthony and Ray Martin (roses); Nigel Coe (gladioli); Clare and Johan Hermans (orchids); Malcolm Hughes (bonsai); June Nash (dahlias); Geoff Oke (fuchsias); Jackie Petherbridge (daffodils); and Raymond Evison and Pamela Spires.

Any suggestions for amendments to *The Horticultural Show Handbook* are welcomed and should be sent to: **thegarden@rhs.org.uk**

GETTING STARTED

This Handbook is intended to give guidance both to those new to staging shows as well as those who have plenty of experience.

If this is the first show you've organised, this section will give some basic pointers and explain how you can use the Handbook to guide you through the process. The guidance can be modified to suit local circumstances.

1 Timing and venue Consider potential clashes with other local events and cropping season. Visit other flower shows to get ideas and information, fix the date well in advance and appoint judges early.

A suitable venue should have plenty of light, be large enough for the anticipated number of exhibits (but not too large), and should have running water.

Once a venue and date have been identified, the show secretary (*See* ***Appoint a show secretary***, *p18*) would normally book the venue, appoint judges and organise other staging materials such as tables, vases, plates, etc.

2 Get a feel for the likely level of exhibitor Many different types of people exhibit at local flower shows. Talk to local groups such as gardening clubs, schools and social clubs to gauge the level of expertise and to establish whether classes for flower arrangement (possibly to be judged under NAFAS rules), domestic produce, novices and children would attract any interest and therefore should be included. Consider also whether novelty classes (such as heaviest marrow, pumpkin, onion, etc) may be appropriate. *See also* ***Clarify who can exhibit***, *p18*.

3 Decide what prizes and awards to give First, second and third prizes are normally awarded for each class with a modest cash award for each. 'Highly Commended' or 'Commended' awards can also be made. 'Best in Section' and 'Best in Show' awards are also often included, as are other special awards. *See* ***Best in show*** *and* ***Best bloom***, *p23*

Societies affiliated to the RHS may apply to the RHS for the grant of a Banksian medal for award at their show. This is available to affiliated societies in each year of their membership provided certain basic criteria are met. The Banksian medal can only be awarded to the winner of the largest total amount of money in prizes, or the highest number of place points, in the whole of the horticultural classes at all the society's shows in a given year. Any competitor who has won the medal in the last two years is not eligible to win (*see also* ***Awards and prize money***, *p28*). A Grenfell medal can be selected instead of a Banksian medal and can be offered for award in connection with the floral arrangement classes of a show. For further details email **affiliated@rhs.org.uk**.

Getting started

RHS Silver and Bronze medals can be purchased by affiliated societies by email at **mailorder@rhs.org.uk**. For further information visit the Support and Resources section of the RHS website at **www.rhs.org.uk/affiliatedsocieties** (click on *Support and resources* then click on *Stationery* under *Information pack*).

Other national plant societies (such as the Daffodil Society, the National Vegetable Society, the National Dahlia Society, the National Chrysanthemum Society, the British Fuchsia Society and the Royal National Rose Society) offer medals in their own specialist sections of affiliated shows.

4 Publicising the show Methods for publicising the show could include:
- Put up posters around the community
- Write a press release and send to your local media
- Put information on your society's website and local websites
- Hire a photographer or get an amateur to take photos at your shows to use in future promotions. Remember to get a permission form signed when photos include subjects under the age of 18.
- Join your local county horticultural federation and publicise your society's activities through its network of local gardening clubs.

The show secretary would typically be responsible for show publicity (*See* **Appoint a show secretary**, *p18*).

5 Public liability insurance Organisers of flower shows are liable for injury suffered by anyone visiting or participating in the show, including members of the public, guests, exhibitors and voluntary staff. If the society does not have public liability insurance cover then the liability lies with the officers of that society who may be proceeded against. It is therefore essential that cover is provided. This may sometimes be provided by the owners of the hall or building in which the show is held. If not, the society must take out a special policy to cover the event.

Societies affiliated to the RHS have access to competitive public liability insurance cover. For further information visit the *Support and Resources* section of the RHS website at **www.rhs.org.uk/affiliatedsocieties**.

6 Other things to organise Now that you have the basics in place, (see **Organising a show**, *pp17–24*) for further details of what you need to do to run a successful show.

7 Rules The rules of the show must be made clear to all exhibitors and judges. The Royal Horticultural Society's rules (*see pp59–61*) are suitable for most shows, with additions or deletions as appropriate. Where specialist awards are given the rules of the appropriate society will need to be followed.

8 Prepare the show schedule   The show schedule should be published well in advance to give exhibitors and judges plenty of time to prepare.

It is particularly important when writing classes for entry to make them as clear and simple to understand as possible to avoid misinterpretation.

See **Writing a show schedule**, *pp27–35* for more detailed information.

9 Giving advice and guidance to exhibitors   Many flower show exhibitors are experienced and know what is expected but novices will probably need some guidance. This handbook contains much detailed advice about how to prepare produce, stage exhibits, how they will be judged, and what the judges are looking for, type by type. It will help to have a copy of this Handbook to hand as a reference for those that need it.

10 On the day of the show   Make sure that there are enough helpers and judges' stewards for the set-up and judging. Ensure the doors open promptly at the published time for staging, and clearly explain to exhibitors how long they have to stage their exhibits.

Take time on the day to make a note of what has worked particularly well and what has not so that you can learn from this experience when you organise your next show.

Getting started

ORGANISING A SHOW

Once the venue has been booked and the date set, there are several other things to do as follows.

1 Clarify who can exhibit   Make it clear whether the show is to be open to amateurs only or also to professionals (*see definitions of amateur and professional in* **Glossary**, *pp186 and 191*).

The definition of amateur allows someone who employs a full-time gardener to compete in the show. If that is not the intention, it is recommended that the schedule states: 'The show is open to amateurs who do not employ a gardener for more than 10 hours per week.'

If professionals are allowed to exhibit, anyone who is employed as a gardener, either full- or part-time, should only be allowed to exhibit produce from their own private garden or allotment in their own name. Produce from an employer's garden must be exhibited in the employer's name.

2 Appoint a show secretary   The show secretary is responsible for the general organisation of the show. Responsibilities would typically include the following points.

In advance:
- Book the venue.
- Do a table layout plan (*see also* **Show table layout**, *p19*) and reserve the tables to be used as show benches.
- Appoint judges. Agree any fee or expenses with the judges at the time of appointment.
- Arrange publicity. *See* **Publicising the Show**, *p13*.
- Arrange for a nominated person, or persons, to receive entries (notifications of intention to exhibit) and entry fees from exhibitors.
- Appoint stewards and ensure they are familiar with their duties (*see* **Appoint stewards**, *p19*).
- Be familiar with the show's rules and take responsibility for their implementation.

On the day of the show:
- Ensure that the show benches are marked out.
- Identify the location of each class by placing cards with the class number. Many societies also have a card with a short description of the class as it appears in the schedule, which is very helpful for the public when the show is open.
- Provide an entry card for each entry (*see* **Entry cards and prize labels**, *p21*) to exhibitors.
- Provide labels for naming each entry (*see* **Labelling exhibits**, *p22*).
- Provide vases, plates, etc if available.
- If any classes (such as onions) have a weight limit, make available an accurate set of scales for the use of exhibitors, stewards and judges, during both staging and judging.
- Ensure that the hall is open and ready for staging at the stated time

and that it remains open until the completion time.
- In case of queries, interpret the wording of the schedule and inform the judges of any relevant decisions before they begin judging.
- Immediately before judging starts, draw together judges and stewards and explain layout, duties and sections (*eg* Vegetables, Fruit or Flowers, etc) to all concerned.
- Deal with protests promptly, consistently and fairly (*see also* **Protests**, *p23*).
- Ensure that prize money is paid promptly after the show, and that any trophies and special prizes reach their respective winners as quickly as possible.

3 Show table layout Traditionally and for the most efficient use of space, show tables are placed in lines with the first row along a wall. At large shows, tiered staging is sometimes used and this can add to the visual effect. Where space allows, circular tables can allow more space for visitors to view the exhibits.

It is important to give thought to table space for each exhibit in each class, as the space required will vary from class to class. As a general guide, a dish of fruit or vegetables will require 30cm of table width, as would a container of a single cut flower. While up to three dishes of fruit or vegetables can be staged directly behind each other, more space should be allowed for flowers, in order that all exhibits can be seen. A class of a single cut flower with three entries might need 45cm of table width if there were two vases at the back and one in front. To calculate how much space is needed for each class, multiply the space required for each entry by the expected or actual number of entries.

In the case of pot-plant classes, it is difficult to be as prescriptive because the size of plants will vary considerably. It is recommended that a maximum pot size is specified in the schedule.

Show organisers have the right to move exhibits if space becomes too crowded. In extreme cases it may be more practical to move an entire class to another staging area. In all cases, always remember to advise the judges. *See also* **Appoint stewards**, *below*.

4 Appoint stewards Stewarding is important and an experienced steward is a great asset to a show. The steward(s) are an important link between the judges, exhibitors and the show secretary, and stewarding is a very good training ground for those who wish to become either exhibitors or judges.

One or more stewards should be appointed to ensure, as far as possible, that all exhibits are according to the schedule and to ensure that judging runs smoothly. A steward should not be asked to officiate in any section where he/she is an exhibitor.

Stewards are responsible for the following:
- Look out for sections where entries are congested. If the space

allotted on the show bench is congested, the steward should report the problem to the show secretary who will adjust the spacing. Any change should be done with extreme care so as not to alter in any way the exhibitor's own staging, and the judges should be informed.
- Assist new exhibitors.
- Ensure that exhibitors put the right exhibit in the right class and ensure that it is staged according to schedule by checking weights, quantities, sizes, container dimensions or space.
- Before judging begins, stewards should ensure that everyone leaves the show venue except those authorised by the show committee to be present during judging. Remove any coverings and ensure each exhibit has its entry card correctly displayed and placed face downwards so that the exhibitor details are not visible.
- Advise judges of any entries that are not according to schedule (NAS). Ensure that judges are aware of any special awards or prizes.
- During judging, stewards should keep at a discreet distance from the judge(s), and should make no comment on the judging except to answer any administrative queries raised by the judge. Stewards should not take part in any technical aspects of judging.
- Stewards may be asked to record results on judges' cards, at the show organiser's discretion.

Once a class has been judged:
- Ensure that every exhibit in that class has been judged.
- Attach the relevant prize sticker to the front of the entry cards but leave the cards face down until all special prizes have been awarded.
- Check that comments on why a class/exhibit has been marked 'not according to schedule' have been made on the appropriate cards.
- Check that points cards, where used, have been completed by the judges.
- Once all judging, including Best Exhibits and any special prizes, has been completed, turn class cards face up to display the prize sticker and exhibitor name.
- When the show is open to the public, keep an eye on the show to prevent theft and the handling of exhibits.

5 Appoint judges   A good judge is impartial, has common sense, is familiar with the kinds and cultivars of the classes to be considered, and has knowledge of the skill required to grow and stage them.

Successful exhibitors often make good judges. Other sources for judges are plant societies and county judges' guilds. To view the RHS Judges Register, visit the *Support and Resources* section of the RHS website at **www.rhs.org.uk/affiliatedsocieties** (click on the link for **lists of speakers and judges** under *Speakers' and Judges' Registers*). Please note that this is a service to assist societies. A judge's appearance on the register does not confer any endorsement by the RHS.

The ideal number of judges is determined by the number of classes and the time available for judging. At smaller shows, two (or

Organising a show

even one) are usually appointed to judge each section or sections. In this case it is a good idea to appoint a referee to give a casting vote if required (see **Referees**, p22).

Judges' responsibilities include the following:
- Assess all exhibits as shown and award prizes as stated in the schedule including any special awards. The judges should decide whether an exhibit in a class is worthy of a prize, but where a trophy is offered for the best exhibit in a section or in the whole show the judges may be asked to make a recommendation for the show committee's consideration.
- Refer to steward and/or show secretary any exhibits that are wrongly staged, incorrectly labelled or not according to schedule. Write a note explaining why an exhibit has been judged to be 'not according to schedule'.
- Be available to receive and act upon protests in a timely fashion.

6 Entry cards and prize labels Each exhibit should have an entry card provided by the show secretary. A suitable size for these is 150×120mm.

Entry cards can be prepared with the exhibitor's name, number and class on the front (with space for a prize sticker if awarded) and the exhibitor's number and class number only on the back. These cards are placed face down beside the entry by the exhibitor, thereby hiding their name. Once judging is complete stewards turn the cards over and attach prize stickers to the front.

Recommended colours for prize labels are red for first prize, blue for second prize and green or yellow for third prize.

Societies that are affiliated to the RHS can purchase entry cards, (above) prize labels and other show stationery from the RHS by email at **mailorder@rhs.org.uk**. For further information visit the Support and Resources section of the RHS website at **www.rhs.org.uk/affiliatedsocieties** (click on *Support and resources* then click on *Stationery* under *Information pack*).

Alternatively each entry can be accompanied by a small card that only has the competitor number and class number. Winning entries should then be given an additional prize card.

7 Labelling exhibits   Shows look better if exhibits are labelled with the name of the cultivar, and it is recommended that the show secretary provides exhibitors with small white cards about 75 × 25mm for this purpose. However, some exhibitors will prepare their own labels in advance of the show and these should also be allowed. Labels are best written or typed in capital letters. *See **Labelling exhibits**, p60.*

8 Recording entries and prizewinners   It is important that accurate records are made of the exhibitors and the judging results.

Judging should be done without knowledge of who the exhibitors are, so it is advisable to allocate each exhibitor a number on receipt of entry. This number and the class entered should be the only information available to judges.

The show organiser should keep an accurate record of all entries made, the points and prize money attained and any special awards given. A database or spreadsheet can be used to record these details in addition to details of the exhibitor, number allocated and classes entered.

There are several ways for judges or stewards to record results, either directly onto the entry cards, onto a result card for each class, or onto a judges' card that has space to list all the results from the classes allocated to them. Below is an example of those available to RHS affiliated societies (*see **Entry cards and prize labels**, p21*).

All cards should be retained by the show organiser as the official record of results.

9 Referees   Some shows, particularly those with strong competition, require final decisions where judgements are in doubt, or where a casting vote is needed. A referee may be appointed for this purpose. In the absence of a referee or other judge, societies should nominate an experienced person who is not exhibiting to arbitrate or confirm unresolved judgements.

10 Best in Show   It is recommended that awards are given for Best Vegetable, Best Flower and Best Fruit exhibits rather than a Best in Show award, as these are easier to judge.

If a Best in Show award is to be made, it is strongly recommended that the award is limited to horticultural exhibits only as it difficult enough for judges to decide between the best flower, fruit and vegetable exhibits, but almost impossible to decide between these and craft, floral art or domestic exhibits. Where there are several judges involved in different sections of the show and a Best in Show award is to be made, each group of judges should decide which, of the exhibits they have judged, is best, and all judges should then seek to agree among themselves which of these exhibits is the Best in Show.

A disqualified exhibit cannot be eligible for Best in Show. Individual vases/dishes in collection classes are not eligible for Best in Section or Best in Show awards as they cannot be considered as exhibits in themselves. (*See however pp147–152 for rules applicable specifically to dahlias.*)

11 Best Bloom   A special award for the Best Bloom shown in the horticultural classes can be offered. The strict definition of a bloom as a single open bloom or flowerhead should be disregarded, so that single spikes or inflorescences of plants such as delphiniums, gladioli and pelargoniums are eligible.

12 Withholding prizes   It is recommended that ***Rule 10*** (*see p61*) regarding the withholding of prizes be adopted. However, in the spirit of encouraging exhibitors, avoid withholding prizes unless necessary to maintain a high standard of exhibits. Do not withhold a prize on the basis that the number of exhibits is low. If an exhibit is worthy of the prize, the prize should be awarded, as it is not the exhibitor's fault that others have failed to exhibit

If none of the exhibits in a class is worthy of first prize, second prize can be awarded to the best exhibit and third prize for that which is next in order of merit. Similarly, if after the first prize in a class has been awarded none of the remaining exhibits is worthy of the second prize, only the third prize should be awarded.

13 Protests   State in the schedule the procedure for making protests including how – usually in writing to the show secretary – and the deadline for making complaints. All complaints should be handled as quickly as possible.

The deadline should be timed so that judges are available to discuss any complaints that concern their decisions or necessitate a review of a class.

Regardless of the deadline, the show committee should be willing to consider a protest that alleges fraud at any time.

Charging a small cash deposit, such as £1, for making a protest may help to deter exhibitors from making groundless complaints. The deposit should be returned if the protest is considered to be justified.

When the show committee of a local horticultural society that is affiliated to the RHS is unable to resolve a problem connected with a show, the show secretary may send details to the Royal Horticultural Society at **affiliated@rhs.org.uk**. Please include a brief summary of the problem, all the relevant facts and, if possible, attach a show schedule.

Organising a show

WRITING A SHOW SCHEDULE

If preparing a schedule for the first time, seek advice from those familiar with organising shows of a similar type. Societies affiliated to the RHS can also seek advice from RHS advisors. Get your society's official contact to email **gardeningadvice@rhs.org.uk** with your society's affiliation number and details of the query.

Decide on entry fees, prize money and awards. Entry fees typically range from no charge to 50p.

Do not seek too many specimens per class. Remember that the quantities suggested in this *Handbook* are for RHS or larger shows.

An example of a basic show schedule is included at the end of this chapter for reference (*see pp35–39*).

What information to include

1 Who's who   At the very least include the name and contact details of the show secretary and the contact for show entries. Judges' names should also be included, if available. Many societies also include the names of society officers.

2 Show rules   It is strongly recommended that the rules under which the show is to be conducted should be clearly stated in full in the schedule. These would normally be the rules set out on *pp59–61*, with such additional rules as may be necessary.

Where certain classes are to be judged according to specialist plant society rules, it is important to mention this in the schedule.

Avoid printing such warnings as 'This rule will be strictly enforced', as this implies that other rules will not be enforced.

3 Show timetable   Include a timetable detailing the following dates and times:
- The deadline for the receipt of entries. *See also* **Deadline for receipt of entries**, *p29*.
- Staging.
- Judging.
- Show open to the public.
- The deadline by which protests should be made.
- Prize-giving, if applicable
- Show closes
- When exhibitors may remove their exhibits.
- The time by which all exhibits and property of exhibitors must be removed.
- The time by which prize money will be paid.

4 Awards and prize money   Include details of any special awards, in addition to prize money. *See also* **Decide what prizes and awards to**

Writing a show schedule

give, p12, *The value of prizes*, p29.

If a Banksian medal is to be awarded you must mention in the schedule that any competitor who has won the Banksian medal at the society's shows in the last two years is not eligible to win the medal.

5 Classes, organised into sections   It is often useful to organise classes into sections. For example, in a spring show:
- Section 1 Cut daffodils
- Section 2 Cut flowers other than daffodils
- Section 3 Pot plants
- Section 4 Novices
- Section 5 Domestic
- Section 6 Children's classes
- Section 7 Handicraft
- Section 4 Photography

This facilitates 'best exhibit' awards.

6 Entry form and entry fee   The entry fee is the charge for entering an exhibit at the show. Typically, entry fees range from no charge to 50p, with junior classes usually free of charge.

Other things to bear in mind

7 Deadline for receipt of entries   In order to encourage the maximum number of entries it is advisable to make the last day for the receipt of entries as late as possible. However, allow enough time between the receipt of entries and the staging of exhibits for administration, table layout and spacing for the various classes to be completed.

The deadline for the receipt of entries should normally be no more than one week before the show, and less if possible. If late entries can be accommodated, include 'late entries will be considered where possible, at the show secretary's discretion' in the schedule.

8 Constitution of exhibits   It is important that the schedule should make clear how many specimens constitute an exhibit. For fruit and vegetables, the quantities ordinarily required at the Royal Horticultural Society's shows are detailed on *pp66–67* and *90–93*. These quantities are also suitable for larger shows. Individual schedule-makers may wish to reduce these to suit the size and scope of their own shows. These quantities can be printed in tables similar to those on *pp37* and *38*, or in the wording of each class.

9 The value of prizes   When an award is to be made to the most successful exhibitor in a show or a section of a show, a competitor's degree of success is usually assessed by giving a point-value to the prizes.

The number of points should be graduated in much the same way as money prizes are graduated, and the point-value of the prizes in the various classes should be stated in the schedule.

As far as possible the relative value of first, second and third prizes should be consistent throughout the schedule.

Thus if a 5:3:2 ratio is adopted and the first prize is, for example, 50p, then the second should be 30p, the third 20p and the fourth (if a fourth prize is awarded) 10p.

The value of the prizes in a class should be related to what is involved in producing the required exhibit.

10 The numbering of classes   To avoid the possibility of confusion, classes should be numbered in consecutive order in the schedule, ie no class number should appear twice.

When a schedule contains two or more sections, leave a gap in the numbering between separate sections to allow classes to be added in sections in future years without entailing all subsequent classes to be renumbered.

For example, if Section 1 ends at Class 15, Section 2 might begin at Class 21 and so on. This would allow anything up to five classes to be added to Section 1 without necessitating the renumbering of the classes in Section 2.

11 The size of pot   It is recommended that a maximum pot size is specified in the schedule. The diameter of a pot or pan is the inside measurement made as close to the top as possible. With square or rectangular pots the area is expressed in square centimetres calculated by measuring straight across the top at right angles to the rim. Where the manufacturer's stamp is embossed on the pot this should be accepted. Where schedule-makers are prepared to admit both circular and rectangular pots in the same class they should state the maximum dimension of both that would be acceptable or give the volume.

12 Multiple-entry classes   Societies may allow multiple-entry classes, which means that exhibitors can make more than one entry in a class, with all entries eligible for prizes. A show schedule can contain one or more multiple-entry classes while retaining the rule of one entry per exhibitor in the rest of the schedule. Ensure that all exhibitors and judges are aware of which classes are multiple-entry and which are not.

If an exhibitor is only eligible to win one prize in a particular class then that class should only allow one entry per exhibitor. This avoids confusion both during judging and for show visitors who may not understand why second and third prizes in such a class have gone to exhibits that are clearly inferior to others that have received no prizes at all.

The use of language when writing a schedule

13 The use of terms Anyone drafting a schedule should become familiar with the meaning of terms in common use and especially with the meaning of 'kinds' and 'cultivars' (varieties). *See definitions of **Kind** and **Cultivar** in the **Glossary**, pp187 and 189.*

14 The use of the terms 'genus', 'species' and 'hybrid' For the purposes of competitions at most horticultural shows the words 'kind' and 'cultivar' are recommended as being not only adequate but also the most easily understood terms to use in the classification of flowers and ornamental plants as well as fruit and vegetables. However, these terms are not always sufficiently precise for alpine, cactus, orchid, succulents, shrub or tree shows. For such competitions the terms 'genus', 'species' and 'hybrid' may also be used.

15 Number of cultivars/kinds In flower classes mixed cultivars are allowed unless otherwise stated. All fruit and vegetable dishes must consist of one cultivar only unless otherwise stated in the schedule.

When writing classes, be clear about the number of cultivars or kinds allowed. For example:
- If the intention is to have a class of three different cultivars of dessert apple, the class should read '**Apples, 3 dessert cultivars, 1 dish of each**'.
- A class reading '**Vegetables, a collection of 4 dishes**' would allow up to four dishes of, for example, potatoes. If different kinds are required, the class should read '**Vegetables, a collection of 4 kinds, 1 dish of each**'.
- If the schedule-maker will allow, for example, two dishes of the same kind of vegetable in the class, the class should read '**Vegetables, a collection of 4 dishes**, not more than 2 dishes of any 1 kind'. This would allow two dishes of the same cultivar of, for example, potato and two dishes of the same cultivar of, for example, cabbage. If this is not intended, the class should read '**Vegetables, a collection of 4 cultivars**, not more than 2 dishes of any 1 kind'.
- A class reading '**Potatoes, 3 dishes**' would allow two or three dishes of the same cultivar to be shown. If different cultivars are required, the class should read '**Potatoes, 3 cultivars**, 1 dish of each'.

In each of the above examples, it is assumed that the schedule will contain a table showing the quantities required. If not, it would be necessary to state the quantities required (*ie* '1 dish of 4 of each').

16 'Distinct', 'similar' and 'dissimilar' It is recommended that the words 'distinct', 'similar' and 'dissimilar' are not used in the descriptions for classes in schedules as they lack precision.

17 'Should' and 'must'   Ensure that the words 'should' and 'must' are used correctly throughout the schedule. 'Should' leaves what follows optional, 'must' makes what follows compulsory.

18 The use of 'and' and 'or'   Schedules sometimes contain classes such as '**Hardy and half-hardy flowers**, 3 kinds, 1 vase of each'. If an exhibitor staged three kinds of hardy flowers it would not be according to the schedule; nor would an exhibit consisting of three kinds of half-hardy flowers.

The class should read '**Hardy and/or half-hardy flowers**, 3 kinds, 1 vase of each' if the intention is to allow all of the following:
- an exhibit consisting solely of hardy flowers;
- an exhibit consisting solely of half-hardy flowers;
- an exhibit consisting partly of hardy and partly of half-hardy flowers.

Things to consider when writing classes for fruits and vegetables

19 The ripeness of fruit   Apples, gooseberries, medlars, pears and quinces may be shown either ripe or unripe, and all other fruits should be ripe, unless specified in the schedule. *See **Ripeness**, p64.*

20 Dual-purpose cultivars of apples   A small number of apple cultivars is considered suitable for exhibiting as either dessert or cooking apples, according to their size (*see **Dual-purpose cultivars**, p65 and Classified List of Fruits, pp81-86*).

21 Any other fruit/vegetable classes   These classes allow exhibitors to show fruit or vegetables that they are not able to enter in any other class in the schedule. The items shown are normally those for which the schedule-makers feel there would be insufficient entries to justify the particular fruit or vegetable having a class of its own.

Within such classes there will probably be a wide diversity of kinds entered, each with a different point value according to the recommendations given on pp66-67. Points are based on the degree of difficulty involved in producing a high-quality crop for the show bench, and it is not desirable that fruits or vegetables that command high points should be judged against those that are easy to grow and therefore command low points. To avoid this situation, schedule-makers are advised to include two 'any other' classes as follows:
- '**Any other fruit/vegetable** with a point value of up to 14, 1 dish.'
- '**Any other fruit/vegetable** with a point value of 15 or more, 1 dish.'

It is appreciated that in small shows on a restricted budget there might only be sufficient prize money and expected exhibitors for one 'any other' class, and where this is the case the judge concerned should be asked to make due allowance for the degree of difficulty of cultivation in his/her assessment. *See also **Any other fruit/vegetable classes**, p56.*

22 Salad vegetables   Refer to ***Salad vegetables** (Glossary, p191)* for details of the kinds that may be used for horticultural shows.

If it is desired that each exhibit in a class should consist of four kinds of such vegetables, then the schedule should call for '**Salad vegetables**, four kinds, 1 dish of each'.

23 Beans   It is often difficult to distinguish climbing from dwarf French beans and they are considered as one kind for exhibition purposes.

24 Beetroot, carrot and potato classes   Exhibitors and judges are often in doubt about the cultivars that may be shown in classes for these vegetables. This uncertainty may in part be caused by different views about the classification of cultivars (either by shape or by colour) and also by the use of wording in classes that is open to a different interpretation. Opinions may differ as to the identity of 'kidney-shaped' potatoes; exhibitors may not know in which classes in a show they should be entered and judges may disqualify them for being in the wrong classes.

Schedule-makers are accordingly advised to adopt as simple wording as possible for beetroot, carrot and potato classes. No attempt should be made to provide separate potato classes for each of the different shapes, nor is a rigid colour classification given. If an exhibitor has specimens of a normally 'coloured' cultivar of potato that show no colour, he/she is able to show them in the 'white' class. Suitable wording where more than one class for beetroot, carrots and potatoes is required is:

Beetroot, cylindrical
Beetroot, globe
Beetroot, long
Carrots, long-pointed
Carrots, stump-rooted
Potatoes, white
Potatoes, coloured

25 Onion classes   Schedule-makers are recommended not to use such wording as 'Onions, spring-sown cultivars', 'Onions, autumn-sown cultivars' or 'Onions, cultivars grown from sets' as these can lead to uncertainty. Difficulties occur when separate classes of this kind are included, as judges are often unable to determine the origin or method of culture of bulbs entered under these headings. When wording onion classes it is advisable to consider examples similar to the following:
Onions, over 250g, 1 dish
Onions, up to 250g, 1 dish
Onions, green salad, 1 dish

26 Tomato classes   Because it is often difficult for judges to distinguish between indoor- and outdoor-grown tomatoes, especially where the latter have had some form of protection such as plastic sheeting, it is suggested that schedule-makers make no distinction between indoor- and outdoor-grown tomatoes.

27 Mixed collection and trug and basket classes   Mixed collection classes have become popular as they demonstrate the all-round ability of the exhibitor. Trug or basket classes improve the attractiveness of the show because the objective is to present fruit and/or vegetables in an attractive way. *See **Mixed collection classes**, p56* and ***Trug and basket classes**, p56*.

Things to consider when writing classes for flowers and ornamental plants

29 Hardy plants   Classes are often provided for 'hardy' plants. A hardy plant is one that is able to survive the average winter when grown in the open without protection.

See **www.rhs.org.uk/plants/pdfs/2012_rhs-hardiness-rating** for more details on the RHS hardiness ratings.

30 Foliage   Unless otherwise stated, in flower classes the use of foliage is optional but if used must be from the kind (genus), but need not be of the cultivar being shown. This should be clarified in the schedule.

31 The wording of classes   It is very important that the wording of classes leaves no doubt as to the schedule-maker's intention for each class. Examples of how to avoid confusion are as follows:

Dahlias
The wording for a vase of five dahlias where the exhibitor can show any number of cultivars of dahlia in one vase should read '**Dahlias, 1 or more cultivars, 1 vase of 5**'.

If you wish to be a little more specialist and limit the class to blooms of cactus or semi-cactus dahlias, the class should read '**Dahlias, cactus and/or semi-cactus, 1 or more cultivars, 1 vase of 5**'.

If you wish to be even more specialist and to allow only small flowers and only 1 cultivar, the class should read '**Dahlias, small cactus or semi-cactus, 1 cultivar, 1 vase of 5**'.

Annuals
Many perennial plants are commonly cultivated as annuals; that is to say, they are raised from seed, flower and then discarded within 12 months. The difficulty of distinguishing between annuals, biennials and perennials is so great that it is recommended that instead of

having a class or classes calling for annuals and/or biennials, such classes should call for 'Flowers raised from seed during the 12 months preceding the Show'. In such a class it would be permissible to exhibit not only true annuals and biennials but also perennials (such as antirrhinums and petunias) which are often cultivated as annuals.

For flowers that are generally grown as annuals, the class should read '**Flowers grown from seed in the preceding 12 months**, 1 vase'. This wording would allow any number of mixed kinds and does not state the quantity required. The class may also state that, for example, three kinds are required and also limit the number of stems to, for example, 10. It would then read '**Flowers grown from seed in the preceding 12 months**, 3 kinds, 1 vase of 10 stems'.

Perennials

Where a class invites the exhibition of a vase of more than one stem of a perennial plant, it is recommended that the wording makes it clear that these should be of similar kinds, for example woody, herbaceous or bulbous. Suitable classes would be:
- '**Hardy herbaceous perennials in bloom**, 1 vase, 5 stems'
- '**Trees and/or shrubs in bloom**, 1 vase, 5 stems'
- '**Hardy herbaceous perennials in bloom**, 3 kinds, 3 vases of 5 stems each'.

If there are individual classes for, for example, roses, and the schedule-maker wishes to exclude them from the more general perennial classes, the class should read: '**Trees and/or shrubs in bloom, excluding roses**, 1 vase, 5 stems'.

Suggested layout /content for a show schedule

The following is an example of what a schedule for a small autumn show might contain.

Page 1: Cover
- Name of society
- Autumn Show Schedule 2016
- Date and location of show

Page 2: Who's who
- Society officers (eg president and other officers)
- Show secretary
- Contact for show entries
- Judges at the show (if available)

Include telephone numbers, email details and addresses for show contacts, with their prior permission.

Page 3: Show rules
- eg RHS rules, amended where necessary and printed in full
- Any other relevant society rules
- If specialist rules are to be followed, state, for example, 'dahlias to be judged by NDS rules and chrysanthemums by NCS rules'

Page 4: Show timetable
- Deadline for the receipt of entries
- Staging times
- Judging times
- Show open times
- Prize-giving, if applicable
- Deadline by which protests should be made
- When exhibits can be removed after show closes
- Deadline by which exhibits must be removed
- When prize money will be paid

Page 5: Awards, points and prize money
*Include quantities required in table format, based on the numbers recommended in this Handbook (See JUDGING FRUITS, **Constitution of dishes**, pp66–67 and JUDGING VEGETABLES, **Constitution of dishes**, pp90–93), with quantities adjusted to suit the size and scope of the show.*

Writing a show schedule

Pages 6–7: Classes arranged in sections

For an autumn (*eg* September) show, suitable classes could include the following:

Section 1: Vegetables

Note: all dishes to consist of one cultivar unless otherwise stated. For number of specimens, see page 5

Class number	Details	Number of specimens
1	**Vegetables, a collection of 4 kinds**, 1 dish of each	See page 5
2	**Onions, over 250g**, 1 dish	3
3	**Onions, up to 250g**, 1 dish	4
4	**Carrots, long pointed**, 1 dish	3
5	**Carrots, stump rooted**, 1 dish	3
6	**Beetroot, globe**, 1 dish	3
7	**Beetroot, long**, 1 dish	3
8	**Potatoes, white**, 1 dish	4
9	**Potatoes, coloured**, 1 dish	4
10	**Tomatoes, large** (75mm in diameter or over), 1 dish	3
11	**Tomatoes, medium** (approximately 60mm in diameter), 1 dish	6
12	**Tomatoes, small-fruited** (no more than 35mm in diameter), 1 dish	9
13	**Tomatoes, truss**	1 truss
14	**Beans, French, climbing or dwarf**, 1 dish	6
15	**Beans, runner**, 1 dish	9
16	**Cucumbers**, 1 dish	2
17	**Courgettes**, 1 dish	3
18	**Marrows**, no longer than 350mm in length	2
19	**Any other vegetable** with a point value of up to 14, 1 dish	See page 5
20	**Any other vegetable** with a point value of 15 or more, 1 dish	See page 5
25	**Heaviest marrow**	1
26	**Longest runner bean**	1

Section 2: Fruit

Note: all dishes to consist of one cultivar unless otherwise stated

Class number	Details	Number of specimens
30	**Fruit, a collection of 3 kinds**, 1 dish of each	See page 5
31	**Apples, dessert**, 1 dish	4
32	**Apples, cooking**, 1 dish	4
33	**Pears, dessert**, 1 dish	4
34	**Plums**, 1 dish	6
35	**Raspberries**, 1 dish	10
36	**Grapes**, 1 dish	1 bunch
37	**Any other fruit** with a point value of up to 14, 1 dish	See page 5
38	**Any other fruit** with a point value of 15 or more, 1 dish	See page 5

Section 3: Flowers

Note: unless otherwise stated, one or more cultivars can be shown in each class

Class number	Details
45	**Flowers grown from seed in the preceding 12 months**, 3 kinds, 1 vase of 6 stems
46	**Hardy herbaceous perennials in bloom**, 1 vase, 5 stems
47	**Trees and/or shrubs in bloom**, excluding roses, 1 vase, 5 stems
48	**Roses, large-flowered**, 1 specimen bloom
49	**Roses, cluster-flowered**, 1 vase, 3 stems
50	**Dahlias, giant or large**, 1 bloom
51	**Dahlias, medium**, 3 blooms
52	**Dahlias, small decorative and/or cactus and/or semi-cactus**, 5 blooms
53	**Dahlias, pompon**, 5 blooms
54	**Chrysanthemums, large flowered, yellow**, 3 blooms
55	**Chrysanthemums, large flowered, white**, 3 blooms
56	**Chrysanthemums, sprays**, 5 stems
57	**Pot plant, foliage plant**, container up to 260mm
58	**Pot plant, flowering plant**, container up to 260mm

Page 8 Entry form with details of entry fee

- Name and year of Show

Name:	
Address:	
Telephone:	
Email:	

I wish to enter the class(es) marked with an 'x' below.
I agree to abide by the rules

Signature:	

Section 1: Vegetables

1		2		3		4		5		6		7		8		9		10	
11		12		13		14		15		16		17		18		19		20	
25		26																	

Section 2: Fruit

30		31		32		33		34		35		36		37		38	

Section 3: Flowers

45		46		47		48		49		50		51		52		53	
54		55		56		57		58									

Total number of entries:	
Total entrance fees @ 20p per entry	

Return this form with entrance fees to:
....

SUGGESTIONS TO EXHIBITORS

1 The schedule   Read the schedule very carefully, including all the rules. If anything is not clear contact the show secretary immediately. Where possible, the solution of problems should not be left until the show day.

2 Dates and times   The dates and times given in the schedule should be carefully noted and adhered to, particularly:
- the deadline for making an entry;
- staging times
- when the show closes, and the time by which exhibitors must have removed their property.

3 Entry form   Ensure your completed entry form is submitted to the right person by the deadline at the latest, but earlier if possible.

4 Selection of cultivars   Some cultivars are naturally better for horticultural-show purposes than others. Exhibitors are advised to visit other shows and to make a note of those cultivars that are successful. Other useful sources of information are experienced exhibitors and national plant societies.

5 Avoid making too many entries   Only put in an entry for classes if you are reasonably sure that you will be able to stage an exhibit in it. Failing to produce the exhibits or late cancellations make it very difficult to layout the staging appropriately, and mean that in some classes the exhibits are crowded and elsewhere there are vacant spaces.

6 Encourage beginners   If you know someone who successfully grows a particular flower, fruit or vegetable for which there is a class, do your best to persuade them to enter.

Experienced exhibitors are encouraged to help new exhibitors where possible, for example by pointing out if they have inadvertently made a mistake (such as staging the wrong number of specimens or omitting to put labels or entry cards in position), help them to put it right or ask the steward to help.

7 Allow ample time for staging   Allow plenty of time for staging exhibits, aiming to finish well ahead of the scheduled time for the completion of staging. Avoid a last-minute rush as this is when mistakes are likely to occur.

8 Labels and entry cards   If you have multiple exhibits it may be prudent to prepare labels in advance in order to save time on the show day. Labels should give the names of the cultivars to be exhibited in block capitals. On arrival at the venue, get your entry cards from the secretary or steward. Place both labels and entry cards by the exhibits in good time, ensuring that they correspond to the

Suggestions to exhibitors

exhibits. Entry cards should be placed face down.

9 'Should' and 'must'   As many schedule-makers inadvertently put 'should' when they mean 'must', if the schedule says 'should' it is wise for an exhibitor to act, if possible, as if the word were 'must'.

10 The number of specimens required   Pay particular attention to the number of specimens for which the schedule asks, as an exhibit consisting of either more or less will be liable to disqualification (NAS: 'not according to schedule').

11 Uniformity of specimens constituting an exhibit   In any competitive exhibit uniformity of all the characteristics of the specimens constituting the exhibit is important. It is unwise to mix, for example, large specimens with others that are smaller as this will weaken the exhibit.

12 Leave the hall for judging   All exhibitors must leave the show venue before judging commences, and must not return until the time fixed for re-admission.

13 The judges' decision   The judges' decision is final and should be accepted with good grace.

14 Protests   If you feel sure that a mistake has been made, a protest should be made in writing to the secretary in accordance with the terms of the show schedule. The final decision should be accepted without question.

If the deadline for the receipt of protests has passed, the judges' decision should be accepted without comment and no action taken.

15 Liability for loss   The organisers usually stipulate in the schedule that exhibits and other property of exhibitors will at all times be at the risk of the exhibitors. It is impossible for the organisers to ensure the safety of exhibitors' property especially when exhibits are being removed at the close of a show. Make arrangements to remove your exhibits during the clearance period, which is usually immediately after the show closes

16 The preparation and presentation of produce at shows   All exhibits should be staged as attractively as possible in accordance with the rules and schedule. In close competition, arrangement may be the deciding factor as this will favourably influence the judges. Always take a few extra specimens to the show in case of accident, and when you have finished staging, check the exhibit is well finished, conforms to the show schedule and is labelled.

17 The presentation of trug and basket classes In these classes, presentation is as important as quality and variety. Take care to comply with any size regulations. *See also **Trug and basket classes**, p56.*

18 The preparation and presentation of fruit (*See also **The preparation and presentation of produce at shows**, p43*) For specialist advice on growing fruit refer to *RHS Grow Your Own Fruit*, by Carol Klein, Mitchell Beazley, 2009, ISBN 9781845334345.

- **Picking** Pick as near to show time as possible, taking care not to damage fruit. Harvest currants, jostaberries and worcesterberries with the strigs intact, choosing the longest strigs with the largest fruits. Pick grapes as a complete bunch and cut each bunch with a piece of lateral shoot on either side of the stalk to form a T-handle. Pick apricots, nectarines and peaches, blueberries and citrus fruits without any attached stalk and stem. Take care not to split the skin in the stalk cavity. Show all other fruits with stalks fresh and intact.

Handle all fruits as little and as gently as possible and by their stalks, if possible, so that the natural bloom is not spoilt. Use scissors to remove soft fruits. Under no circumstances should fruit be polished.

- **Selection** The desirable qualities of each kind of fruit are set out in *Judging Fruits* (*see pp63–86*). Choose only fruits as near to perfection as possible. The fruits should be fresh, uniform, free from blemish and characteristic in shape and colour. Refer to the show schedule to see what is required, but pick more than is necessary so that reserves are available when staging. Do not use overripe fruits. Unripe fruits are not ideal except where allowed in certain classes (*see **Ripeness**, p64*). Figs with signs of splitting and gages with signs of slight shrivelling can be exhibited as this is a sign of ripeness.
- **Packing** Pack carefully bearing in mind that soft fruits may be damaged by their own weight; avoid packing too many in one container. Keep in a cool place.
- **Presentation and staging** Aim for a neat, attractive presentation, as symmetrical as possible. Do not polish the fruits.

Apples and similar-shaped fruits should be staged with the eye uppermost, stalk end downwards, placing one fruit in the centre and the remainder around it. The centre fruit can be raised. Do not cut the stalks.

Berries, excluding blueberries, look most attractive if placed in lines. The stalks and calyces should look green and fresh and all point one way. Reject malformed and damaged fruits. Blueberries should be staged around the perimeter of a plate.

Worcesterberries and currant × gooseberry hybrids should have strigs intact and laid roughly parallel, the bottom of the strigs to the front of the plate. Mound the fruit in the centre.

Grapes are usually shown in one of two ways. Unless some other method of staging is specified or permitted by the schedule, glasshouse grapes should be staged on stands and should be pulled well up onto the board. Outdoor grapes grown for winemaking or dessert may be shown on plates.

Most pears, pear-shaped quinces and figs are best arranged around the perimeter of the plate with the stalks towards the centre.

Plums, cherries and similar-shaped fruits are best laid out in lines across the plate. It is important that the bloom is not disturbed and the stalks are intact.

19 The preparation and presentation of vegetables (See also *The preparation and presentation of produce at shows, p43*)

For specialist advice on growing vegetables for shows refer to the National Vegetable Society at www.nvsuk.org.uk

Where necessary, vegetables should be carefully washed to remove soil but in no circumstances should oils or similar substances be applied in an attempt to enhance their appearance. Wash with a soft cloth and plenty of water: brushing will damage the skin and spoil the appearance of the exhibit. Retain the natural 'bloom' wherever possible. All vegetables should be handled carefully during preparation.

Vegetables should be staged as attractively as possible on plates or direct on the table.

Artichokes, globe   Disbud the lateral heads leaving only the large main head. Stage heads on a plate, stalks to the centre.

Asparagus peas, mangetout and snap peas   Select fresh pods of good colour, that snap easily, and of a size appropriate for the cultivar, approximately 30-40mm with stalk attached.

Aubergines   Cut the fruit carefully and stage on a plate, taking care to retain the natural skin condition.

Beans, broad; French, climbing or dwarf; runner; and shelling, other than broad (*eg* borlotti and similar types)   Exhibit fresh pods of uniform colour. Stage a uniform-sized exhibit with pods arranged on a plate or directly on the bench; in a line with the tail ends facing the front. With all beans it is advisable to check one or two spare pods to assess the condition and interior freshness. Cut all pods from the vine with scissors, ensuring that each pod has a portion of stalk.

Beetroot   Select roots of even size; for globe beetroot, between 60 and 75mm; for long beetroot as for parsnips (*see p48*); and for cylindrical cultivars, roots approximately 150mm in length. Avoid specimens with poor skin colour at the base of the root or that do not have a single small taproot. Small side roots should be removed. Take care in washing as all marks will show up clearly after a few hours. Trim foliage to approximately 75mm.

Brussels sprouts   Cut from the main stem with a knife, all stalks to be approximately the same length. Choose tightly closed sprouts of uniform size. Do not remove too many outer leaves, otherwise depth of colour is reduced.

Cabbages   Choose solid heads of equal size, clean and with good waxy bloom. Take care not to mark the bloom. Reject split specimens and any damaged by pests. Remove only a minimum of outer leaves. Stage with approximately 75mm of stalk remaining and heads towards the front.

Carrots Choose firm, fresh, blemish-free specimens of good even colour and uniformity, without discoloration at the top. Carrots should have the soil or growing medium soaked at the time of lifting to minimise damage to the root. Cut off the foliage to approximately 75mm. Lay side by side in a triangular formation with the root end facing the front.

Cauliflowers, calabrese and broccoli, coloured-headed Reject pest-damaged, discoloured, split, loose or uneven-sized heads. Stage with approximately 75mm of stalk remaining. Just prior to staging, trim back leaves so that they match the level of the outside of the curd. Cover white curds with clean paper or cloth to exclude light, but remove immediately before the start of judging.

Celery Choose only heads that have no diseased or pest-damaged foliage and that have not been damaged by slugs. Reject specimens with heart rot or with flowerheads forming. Place a tie round the base of the leaves to prevent breaking and clean by a continuous flushing with water; ensure all pests are removed. Before staging, neatly trim off the roots, leaving a pointed butt end. In dish classes where few heads are required, lay them flat on the show bench. In collection classes, enhance specimens by displaying on a backboard. To exclude the light, cover with clean paper or damp cloth, which must be removed immediately prior to judging.

Courgettes Select young, tender, shapely and uniform fruits approximately 150mm in length and approximately 25–35mm in diameter, in any colour, or in the case of round cultivars approximately 75mm in diameter. Stage flat with or without flowers still attached.

Cucumbers Fruits should be completely matched and of a good, fresh green colour. The flower end should be completely developed, the barrel well shaped and with a short handle. Display specimens flat on the show bench. It is not necessary that flowers remain attached. Cucumbers grown under protection should be 250mm or more in length. Outdoor-grown cucumbers can be smaller.

Fennel, Florence Roots should be neatly trimmed off and foliage trimmed back to approximately 75–100mm, but with terminal foliage retained.

Flower sprout, Petit Posy Cut main stem with a sharp knife, trim all the stalks to be of the same length. Choose nice open sprouts of similar size with good colour and no pest damage. Exhibit in a shallow bowl of water to retain freshness. Cover dish with damp paper towel to reduce moisture loss while staging. Remove for judging.

Garlic Clean off all soil fragments, dry completely. Reduce the dried stem to approximately 25mm and remove the roots. Stage bulbs as complete specimens; do not divide into segments (cloves).

Kale It is recommended that leaves are exhibited in vases to maintain freshness.

Suggestions to exhibitors

Kohlrabi   Choose tender, fresh specimens of a size according to cultivar. Trim roots neatly. Cut side foliage back to approximately 20mm and retain the terminal foliage. Stage in clean condition, but do not wash, and retain the natural bloom.

Leeks   Specimens should be uniform in length, in good condition and solid (ie firm and compact throughout the length of the barrel) with a good, uniform blanch that is not bulbous at the base. Avoid excessive stripping of outer leaves, otherwise unsightly ribbing is exposed. In dish classes, preferably stage the leeks to lie flat on the bench with the roots to the front, neatly teased out and well cleaned. Ensure that stem (barrel), leaves (flags) and roots (beard) are flushed clean with tapwater, which should not be allowed to run between the leaves leaving unsightly soil particles. Avoid soft, discoloured specimens, or evidence in the stem and leaves of rust disease. Place specimens in collections vertically on a backboard, complementing celery, where shown, in length. Bind in the leaves to an appropriate length. Reject specimens that show evidence of the formation of a flowerhead. Some schedules have classes for intermediate leeks, ie where the blanch to the tight button is more than 150mm and less than 350mm. Pot leeks call for a 150mm maximum blanch from root base to 'tight button', ie the point where the lowest leaf breaks the circumference of the blanched stem. Size should be of a maximum cubic capacity.

Lettuce   Lift with roots intact in the evening or early morning when the leaves are turgid. Fresh heads of uniform and attractive colour are essential. Roots should be washed, wrapped in moist tissue, inserted in a plastic bag and neatly tied. Wash, avoiding soil particles collecting between the leaves. Remove damaged outside leaves, and stage laid on the show bench with the hearts facing the front.

Marrows   Choose tender, young, uniform fruits, which should be less than 350mm long or, in the case of round cultivars, approximately 500mm in circumference. Old, mature fruits that are not suitable for table use should be excluded. Wipe clean and stage directly on the show bench.

Onions   Uniform, well-ripened bulbs of good colour are required. Avoid soft, stained specimens with thick, immature necks. Do not over-skin. The tops should be neatly tied and the roots neatly trimmed back to the basal plate. Onions are often staged on rings or soft collars. Pickling onions should not exceed 30mm in diameter nor should the necks be tied. Onions on ropes should contain 8 onions neatly presented, either tied or plaited. Check quantities.

Onions, green salad   Stage plants with foliage and roots attached, and well washed.

Oriental brassicas, heading types   Choose representative specimens of equal size, clean and with good bloom. Reject damaged heads. Display with roots intact, well washed, wrapped in moist tissue, inserted in a plastic bag and neatly tied.

Parsley   Show only by itself as a herb. It may be used as a garnish for a collection of vegetables, but should receive no points in this case except under the heading of 'arrangement'.

Parsnips   Roots should be straight and of good length, evenly tapered and well developed. Great care should be taken in lifting the roots, as bruising by fingers and scratching by soil particles will show later. Parsnips should have the soil or growing medium soaked at the time of lifting to minimise damage to the root. Wash thoroughly with clean water. Cut off the foliage to approximately 75mm. Lay side by side in a triangular formation with the root end facing the front.

Peas   Pods should be uniform in length and in good condition. Judges will open and check pods during their examination. When cutting from the vine retain the waxy bloom intact without finger marks. Gather by cutting with scissors and with approximately 25mm of stalk, holding the pod at all times by this. Holding pods up to a strong light will detect internal damage and reveal the number of peas in the pod. Arrange on a plate or directly on the bench, in a line with the tail ends facing the front.

Peppers, sweet and hot (chilli)   Select fruit of the right shape, size and colour for the cultivar. The exhibit should be uniform in colour. Fruit may be shown immature but fully formed, usually green, or at the mature or coloured stage. Mature specimens are to be preferred.

Potatoes   Select medium-sized specimens, generally between 200g and 250g. Choose equally matched tubers with shallow eyes. Freedom from skin blemishes that may be caused by pests, diseases or careless handling is important. Very carefully wash the tubers in clean water with a soft sponge – do not use a coarse cloth or brush. Stage on plates with the rose end outwards; cover with a cloth to exclude light until judging commences.

Pumpkins   Show a well-formed specimen, mature and of good colour.

Radishes, small salad   The body of the radish should be fresh, firm, medium-sized, young, tender and brightly coloured. It should be free from blemishes and with foliage trimmed to approximately 30mm. Dig at the last possible moment to retain maximum turgidity. Cut spare specimens to check internal condition.

Rhubarb   Stalks should be fresh, straight, long and tender with well-developed colouring. Cut off top foliage of natural rhubarb leaving approximately 75mm from start of leaf stalks. Do not cut off foliage of forced rhubarb. Wipe stalks clean and trim off any bud scales at the bottom.

Salsify and scorzonera   Roots should be clean and straight and with approximately 75mm of leaf stalk remaining.

Shallots   Stage as separate bulbs and not as clusters. Bulbs should be thoroughly dried, free from staining and loose skins. Cut off roots to the basal plate and tie the tops neatly. Stage on dry sand or similar material which should (preferably) be of a contrasting colour and piled on the plate slightly to raise the centre. Shallots for pickling

must not exceed 30mm in diameter.
Spinach, spinach beet, chard (including white and coloured cultivars)
Use large, very fresh, thick, undamaged, well-coloured leaves and stalks. Mixed colours of leaves and stems will be permitted if from a mixed variety. Defer gathering until the last possible moment to retain turgidity and so that there is as little delay as possible before staging. Leaves should be complete with a neatly trimmed stalk. Display for effect in a vase, with water. Careful handling is essential.
Squash, summer Select young, tender, shapely and uniform fruits, normally not more than five days after flowering. Cut fruit from the vine, taking care not to mark the tender flesh. Stage as for courgettes.
Squash, winter Select fully coloured, mature fruit, with few blemishes, and of a size according to cultivar. Retain the stalk.
Sweet corn Cobs of uniform size with fresh green husks should be displayed with approximately one quarter of the grain exposed by pulling down sharply, from the tip to the base. The best cobs are filled to the tip with straight rows of tender grains. The grains should be well-filled, not shrivelled. The stalks should be trimmed.
Tomatoes Select fruit of the right shape, size and colour for the cultivar. Fruit should not be overripe or with hard 'green back' colouring around the calyx. Aim for a uniform firm set of ripe fruits with firm, fresh calyces. Stage on a plate, calyx uppermost.
Tomatoes, truss Cut the truss from the plant carefully, as near the main stem as possible. Both mature and immature fruits may be shown but at least one third of the fruits should be fully ripe, displaying the natural colour for the cultivar.
Turnips and swedes Select fresh, tender, disease-free roots of a size and shape according to cultivar, but not over-large, and with a small taproot. Wash carefully, remove dead foliage. Cut a spare root to check inside for disease and condition.

20 The preparation and presentation of flowers   (See also *The preparation and presentation of produce at shows*, p43)
• **Cutting** The ideal time to cut flowers is in the evening (or early morning if that is not possible). Flowers should be cut with as much stem as possible, making a slanting cut to assist the uptake of water. Sometimes flowers (such as chrysanthemums and penstemons) may not absorb water easily and the stems can be slit upwards (approximately 75mm) under water to assist. After cutting, remove sideshoots, unwanted buds and lower leaves and place the flowers upright in a container of clean deep water. It is better for this to be done overnight if possible, and then the container of flowers should be placed in a cool dark room. To save time at the show, labels showing the name of the cultivar can be written in advance, using cards or paper.
• **Transit to a show** Many exhibitors carry their exhibits in vases in 'milk crates', making sure that packing prevents excessive movement

of each flower during transportation. If using supports for flower stems, they should be removed prior to staging. It is useful to take spare containers to assist when staging.

- **Staging** Carefully unpack each flower and place in a spare container. Fill each exhibition vase with fresh water prior to staging. If using oasis, place in position as early as convenient. Stage each vase carefully, ensuring that the stem is neither too long nor too short and that damaged leaves are removed. If inexperienced, look at the experienced exhibitors' staging, particularly height and spacing of blooms. Blooms should all face the same direction unless 'all round effect' is required by the class. Place exhibits in the classes entered and place labels with the exhibit.
- **Pot plants** 'All-round effect' is important in most pot plants (*see also p162–163*) and plants should be turned every few days. This is particularly important in the few days before a show. If necessary, flowers and leaves should be gently 'teased' out so that the plant is displayed at its best. Any damaged foliage or flowers can be carefully removed. Take care during transit that the plant arrives undamaged. Final preparation should involve removing any faded foliage and flowers back to the base, and ensuring that the container is clean. Stage the plant so that its best side is towards the front, and place the label nearby.

Suggestions to exhibitors

SUGGESTIONS TO JUDGES

Judging is not, and never can be, a precise science. It is important that the following judging rules and recommendations are followed in order that, wherever possible, the same result is reached irrespective of who is the judge.

1 Judging engagements Judges should seek written confirmation of all engagements, and the fees or expenses agreed. Once an engagement has been accepted it is up to the judge to suggest a suitable replacement if it is found that he/she is unable to fulfil the engagement.

2 The schedule Before going to the show judges should read the schedule carefully, make themselves familiar with any special or unusual stipulations that it contains and should ensure that they have all the equipment necessary to judge effectively.

3 Punctuality Judges should make every effort to reach the show at the time arranged and if possible to inform the show secretary of any unforeseen delays.

4 When to enter the show venue Judging should be carried out without knowing the identity of the exhibitors. For this reason and as far as possible, judges should not enter the show venue until staging has been completed and exhibitors have left.

5 Rules Judges should familiarise themselves with the rules by which they are judging as very occasionally rules for judging different flowers, fruits or vegetables may contradict each other.

6 Familiarisation with the show The standard of judging should reflect the standard of the show.

7 Order of Judging Some flowers change condition rapidly due to light or temperature and should be judged first. For example, tulips in spring shows, roses in summer shows and dahlias in autumn shows.

8 Procedure in judging a class Before judging individual classes, the judge should establish the standard of the whole show, before briefly examining each section he/she is judging to identify obvious errors, which should be pointed out to the steward. Each exhibit in a class should then be examined in detail.

9 Personal preferences and prejudices A judge should put personal preferences to one side when judging and only consider the merits and defects of the exhibit according to the guidance given in this *Handbook*.

Suggestions to judges

10 Exhibits should be judged as seen   Exhibits should be judged according to how they look at the time of judging. The judge should not take into account how the exhibit may look before or after that time.

11 Speed in judging   Judges should devote sufficient time to each class to assess each exhibit's merits and faults. Be thorough, but not to the extent that the opening of the show is delayed.

12 The opinion of the majority must prevail   The judging of horticultural exhibits is not and never can be an exact science and a decision may hinge on something about which two opinions are possible. When judges disagree with each other, each judge's reasons should be heard but the opinion of the majority must be accepted. If there is an equal number of judges a referee or another judge should be called upon to make the casting vote. Sometimes reconsideration of individual views can be changed by breaking down the individual attributes according to the pointing system.

13 Exhibits that appear to be of equal merit   A close examination of exhibits that appear to be of equal merit will usually reveal something that warrants the placing of one exhibit ahead of the other.

Where an award is to be given in collection classes using points, and two exhibits obtain the same number of points, it should be possible to re-examine the exhibits and add or subtract half a point.

14 Withholding prizes   Judges should award all prizes where possible. *See also* **Withholding prizes**, *p23*.

15 Pointing exhibits   There is usually insufficient time to point all exhibits. If a class is decided by points (*eg* a collection class) it is recommended that the pointing cards are left with the exhibits.

16 Exhibits that are 'not according to schedule'   Show organisers are recommended to appoint stewards to ensure, as far as possible, that all exhibits are according to schedule. Even when this is the case, there may be exhibits that do not conform to the schedule and judges should reject them.

In these cases, the judges should write on the exhibit's card 'not according to schedule' together with a note of the reason(s).

If all or most of the exhibits in a class do not comply with the schedule due to a misunderstanding, the judge should draw this to the attention of the show secretary.

A disqualified exhibit cannot be eligible for consideration for Best in Show.

17 Collection classes Judges should examine all exhibits in as much detail as possible, without dismantling the exhibit to such an extent that it cannot be reassembled.

18 Mixed collection classes Classes, such as 'Flowers, 1 vase; Fruit, 1 dish: Vegetables, 1 dish' have become popular in some shows. The judges for such classes often have different specialisations, and it is suggested that each item is judged using the merits and defects in this *Handbook*, but with the points value for each item adjusted to 20.

19 Trug and basket classes It is recommended that these are judged, not by following the points recommendations made elsewhere in this *Handbook*, but with 20 points being given to each of quality, variety and presentation.

20 Any other fruit/vegetable classes When judging classes for 'any other' fruits or vegetables, the pointing system should not be used as this is only intended for judging like against like. A dish of well-grown fruits or vegetables normally receiving low points should be preferred to an indifferent dish of vegetables or fruits normally receiving high points.

Unusual fruit and vegetables should be considered equally with more common cultivars or kinds.

21 Uniform treatment of exhibits Judges are reminded to treat all exhibits in a uniform manner. For example, in a runner bean class at least one pod in every entry should be snapped across, not only for those entries that appear to be in the running for prizes. Omission may leave an exhibitor believing that his/her exhibit has not been judged. Everything possible must be done to give the exhibitor confidence. At smaller shows, if the judge feels able to make a decision without breaking any exhibit, this is acceptable.

22 Cutting fruit or vegetables Judges may cut fruits or vegetables to determine the internal condition, but this should be rarely necessary.

23 Size Judges should remember that, whilst size is an important factor, the largest exhibit is not always the best. *See **Size, Judging Fruits, Size** p64 and **Judging Vegetables, Size** p90.*)

24 Judging single specimens of fruit or vegetables When only one specimen is shown, maximum points for uniformity should be included.

25 Pest infestations Any plant with a bad pest infestation should be removed from the show.

Suggestions to judges

26 Exhibit labels Correct wrong plant names and, where known, add the name to a label that bears the words 'NAME UNKNOWN'.

27 Provide feedback If applicable, advise the show secretary after the show of ways in which the schedule could be improved.

RULES

The following rules have been adapted from those that apply to all Royal Horticultural Society competitions and are suitable for incorporation in the schedules of many local flower shows.

If these, or other plant society rules, are adopted and not printed in full in the schedule, the schedule should make it clear how exhibitors that are unfamiliar with those rules can access them.

Show organisers may also want to adopt their own rules.

1 Acceptance of entries   The show committee reserves the right to refuse any entry and, in the event of such refusal, is not to be required to give any reason or explanation.

2 Eligibility of exhibitors   On all questions regarding the eligibility of an exhibitor the decision of the show committee shall be final.

3 Exhibits must be the property of the exhibitor   All exhibits must be the property of the exhibitor, and must have been grown from seed by the exhibitor or been in his/her possession or cared for by him/her for at least two months prior to the date of the show. This ruling does not apply to floral arrangement classes where exhibitors are allowed to use plant material that has not been grown by themselves.

4 Number of entries allowed   Only one person per household may exhibit in any class with produce from the same garden and/or allotment, unless the exhibit is entered in joint names.

5 Constitution of an exhibit   Each exhibitor is responsible for compliance with the rules governing each class entered. If an error is noticed at any time it may be corrected by the stewards, but they are under no obligation to do so.

6 Labelling exhibits   Every exhibit should be correctly and clearly labelled with the correct name of the cultivar written in block capitals. Errors in naming may not disqualify, except where the judges consider that an exhibitor is showing one cultivar under two or more names. If the cultivar name is unknown the label should read 'NAME UNKNOWN'. When an unnamed seedling is shown it should be labelled 'SEEDLING'. Correct and clear labelling may be viewed as an advantage in close competition.

7 Constitution of fruit and vegetable dishes   Each dish must consist of one cultivar (variety) only. The numbers of specimens constituting dishes in a collection of fruit or vegetables must be those specified in the single-dish classes.

8 Layout of exhibits The show committee's officers may direct the placing of all exhibits.

9 Only one prize in a class No exhibitor may be awarded more than one prize in any one class unless permitted by the schedule. (*See also **Multiple-entry classes**, p30*)

10 Prizes may be withheld Prizes need not be awarded to exhibits considered to be below standard.

11 Exhibits not according to schedule Any exhibit that does not conform to the wording of the schedule should be disqualified and a judge must write on the entry card 'Not according to schedule' (NAS) in addition to a note as to why it is marked NAS. A vase/dish from a disqualified collection is not eligible for a best dish award (*but see dahlias, p150*).

12 Decisions The decisions of the judges as to the relative merit of the exhibits shall be final. Any other points in dispute will be decided by the show committee and/or its appointed referees, particularly cases of disputed nomenclature, when specimens may be withdrawn for further inspection.

13 Protests Any protest must be made in writing and delivered to the secretary by the time stated in the schedule.

14 Alteration of exhibits After judging has taken place no exhibit or part of an exhibit may be altered or removed until the end of the show, except by special permission of the secretary.

15 Liability for loss All exhibits, personal property, etc., will be at the risk of the exhibitors and the show committee will not be liable for compensation for loss or damage. Exhibitors will be wholly responsible for all claims made by their own employees under the Common Law or under any statute for compensation arising out of or in the course of such employment for injury or otherwise. The show committee has no responsibility to any but its own employees.

16 Right to inspect gardens of exhibitors In order to be satisfied that the conditions governing competitive exhibits are fulfilled, the show committee reserves the right for its official representative to visit by appointment, before or after any show, gardens from which plants, flowers, fruit or vegetables have been entered for competition. If it is decided to exercise that right for one or more exhibitor, it does not mean that the gardens of any other exhibitors need be visited.

JUDGING FRUITS

When assessing the relative merits of dishes of most fruits the following features should be considered: condition; uniformity; size; colour.

A dish must consist of one cultivar only.

Condition

Merits All fruits should be clean, fresh and blemish-free with attractive, naturally produced colour with the natural bloom intact.

Ripeness Apples, gooseberries, medlars, pears and quinces may be shown either ripe or unripe and all other fruits should be ripe, unless otherwise specified in the schedule. Where classes for apples, gooseberries, medlars, pears or quinces are included and the schedule does not specify that the fruit must be ripe, preference should always be given to cultivars in season rather than to larger or more showy cultivars that have been picked prematurely. Over-ripeness will be regarded as a defect in any fruit.

Stalks Apricots, nectarines, peaches, blueberries and citrus fruit are all shown without stalks. All nuts are shown without stalks or husks. All other fruits should be shown with stalks fresh and intact.

Defects Over-ripeness, shrivelling (except in gages), malformations, decay, splitting (except in figs), blemishes, bruises or other injury, imperfect bloom or absence of stalks or eyes except where allowed (see **Stalks**, *above*).

Uniformity All the specimens exhibited on a dish should be uniform, *ie* alike in size, condition, form and colour. When only one specimen is shown and points for uniformity are available, those points should be excluded.

Size All fruits, except dessert apples, should be above the average size for the cultivar but enormous specimens should not be preferred, as beyond a certain point size may become a defect, especially in dessert fruits. An exhibit of a cultivar that is naturally large should not be preferred to an exhibit of a cultivar that is naturally small, unless the exhibit of the larger cultivar is superior to that of the smaller cultivar in other respects. In cooking (but not dessert) apples and in all other fruits, whether dessert or cooking, provided that the contents of two dishes are equal in all other respects, including uniformity, the dish with the larger specimens relative to average cultivar size should be preferred. In grapes and currants, provided that two exhibits are equal in all other respects, including uniformity, large bunches should be preferred.

In dessert apples, it is recommended that the fruits should be

Judging fruits

between 60 and 80mm in diameter, but the judge should make allowances for the fact that some cultivars are inherently small, whereas others are naturally large, typically the triploids. Examples of inherently small or large dessert apples are:

Small 'Margil', 'Pitmaston Pine Apple', 'Sunset' and 'Winston'.
Large 'Belle de Boskoop', 'Blenheim Orange', 'Charles Ross', Crispin ('Mutsu'), 'Gascoyne's Scarlet', 'Jonagold', 'Jupiter', 'Reinette du Canada', 'Rival' and 'Wealthy'.

Dual-purpose cultivars A small number of of apple cultivars is considered suitable for exhibiting as either dessert or cooking apples, according to their size. Such cultivars are denoted on pp81–84 by the words '**small** fruits' or '**large** fruits' after the cultivar name. Ideally, when these cultivars are shown as dessert apples, they should not exceed the optimum size of 75mm in diameter. When shown as cooking apples ideally they should comfortably exceed the minimum size of 80mm. Over-size or under-size would not disqualify an exhibit.

It should be noted that, in collection classes, the same cultivar cannot be shown as both a dessert and a cooking apple.

Colour Attractive, naturally produced colour. The natural bloom should be preserved and colour resulting from the removal of natural bloom or any form of polishing is considered to be a defect.

The classification of dessert and cooking cultivars of fruits Apples, pears and plums must be shown as dessert or cooking cultivars in accordance with the *Classified list of fruits (see p81–86)*, unless the schedule provides otherwise. A new cultivar not listed may be shown and if necessary a classification as to whether it is dessert or culinary may be obtained from the Society beforehand. *See also **Dual-purpose cultivars**, above.*

Constitution of dishes

Unless otherwise specified it is suggested that the numbers given below are used for larger shows. Smaller shows should adopt smaller quantities, half the quantity stated (rounded up) being the recommended minimum, and quantities instead of weights where weights are specified.

	Number of specimens required	Maximum points for a dish *
Apples, cooking	6	18
Apples, dessert	6	20
Apricots	6	16
Apriums	6	16
Blackberries and hybrid cane fruits	20	12
Blueberries	dish of 200–250g	12
Cape gooseberries	20	10
Cherries, sour	20	12
Cherries, sweet	20	16
Citrus fruits, kumquats and calamondins	9	18
Citrus fruits, other than kumquats and calamondins	3	18
Currants, black and other than black	dish of 200–250g	12
Damsons and bullaces	9	8
Figs	5	16
Gooseberries	20	12
Grapes, glasshouse	1 bunch	20
Grapes, outdoor	2 bunches	16
Huckleberries and garden huckleberries	dish of 200–250g	8
Japanese loquats	10	10

* The exhibition value of any kind of fruit is governed by the difficulty of producing a perfect dish.

Judging fruits

	Number	Points *
Kiwi fruits (Chinese gooseberries)	6	12
Medlars	10	8
Melons	1	18
Melons, horned (kiwanos)	2	12
Mulberries	20	8
Nuts	dish of 425–450g	12
Passion fruits (*Passiflora* species)	5	12
Peaches and nectarines	5	20
Pears, Asian	6	20
Pears, cooking	6	18
Pears, dessert	6	20
Persimmons (*Diospyros kaki*)	5	12
Pineapple guavas (*Acca sellowiana*)	5	10
Pineapples	1	20
Plums, cooking	9	14
Plums, dessert and gages	9	16
Pluots	9	16
Quinces	6	12
Raspberries	20	12
Strawberries	15	16
Strawberries, alpine (*Fragaria vesca*)	25	8
Tamarillos or tree tomatoes (*Solanum betaceum*)	9	12
Worcesterberries and currant × gooseberry hybrids eg jostaberries and chuckleberries	dish of 200–250g	12

Please *see Other fruits, p80* for maximum points for a dish, and a guide to number of specimens for those fruits only infrequently seen on the show bench.

Alphabetical list of fruits

Alpine strawberries
See *Other fruits*, p80.

Apples, cooking
Merits   Large, shapely, solid fruits with undamaged eyes, stalks intact and clear unblemished skins of a colour characteristic of the cultivar.
Defects   Fruits that are small, misshapen, overripe or soft or that have damaged eyes or lack stalks or have any blemish, including evidence of any physiological disorder such as bitter pit or glassiness.
Advice to judges   Ensure that all stalks are present and that the fruits are of a good size.

Condition	6 points
Uniformity	6 points
Size	6 points
TOTAL	18 points

Apples, dessert
Merits   Optimum-sized (*see pp64–65 for a full definition of size*), shapely fruits with eyes and stalks intact and clear unblemished skins of the natural colour characteristic of the cultivar.
Defects   Fruits that are too small or too large, misshapen, overripe or soft or that have damaged eyes or lack stalks or are not well-coloured, or have any blemish, including evidence of any physiological disorder such as bitter pit or glassiness.
Advice to judges   Ensure that the fruits are not much larger or much smaller than 75mm in diameter. Ensure that stalks are present.

Condition	6 points
Uniformity	6 points
Suitability of size	4 points
Colour	4 points
TOTAL	20 points

Judging fruits

Apricots

Merits Large, highly coloured, clear-skinned, ripe fruits free from any blemish.

Defects Fruits that are small or poorly coloured or that lack clear skins or that are unripe or overripe or have any blemish.

Advice to judges Apricots are shown without stalks. Handle fruits carefully to avoid bruising.

Condition	4 points
Uniformity	4 points
Size	4 points
Colour	4 points
TOTAL	16 points

Apriums

Judged to the same standards as *Apricots, above*.

Blackberries and hybrid cane fruits

eg **boysenberries, Japanese wineberries, loganberries, sylvanberries; also tayberries**

Merits Large, ripe fruits, of good colour, free from blemishes, in good condition, with fresh calyces, and having stalks.

Defects Fruits that are small, unripe or overripe, of a dull colour, not in good condition or that have blemishes due to insect damage or imperfect fertilisation or that lack stalks.

Advice to judges Handle the fruit carefully, by the stalk. Take care when handling the stalks of thorny cultivars.

Condition	4 points
Uniformity	3 points
Size	3 points
Colour	2 points
TOTAL	12 points

Blueberries

Merits Large, ripe fruits of good colour and bloom, free from blemishes, in good condition.

Defects Fruits that are small, unripe or overripe, of a dull colour, not in good condition, blemished or with imperfect bloom.

Advice to judges Blueberries should be shown as single berries. Handle the fruits as little as possible to avoid damaging the bloom.

Condition	4 points
Uniformity	3 points
Size	3 points
Colour	2 points
TOTAL	12 points

Boysenberries
See *Blackberries and hybrid cane fruits*, p69.

Bullaces
See *Damsons and bullaces*, p72.

Cape gooseberries
Merits Calyces intact, dry, ochre-coloured, clean, blemish-free, containing large, ripe, unblemished fruits of good colour.
Defects Calyces immature, damaged, blemished, containing small or unripe or overripe fruits of poor colour or condition.
Advice to judges Open the calyces of one or more specimen in each exhibit to ensure the fruit is in good condition and of reasonable size.

Condition	4 points
Uniformity	2 points
Size	2 points
Colour	2 points
TOTAL	10 points

Cherries, sour
Merits Large, ripe fruits, of brilliant colour, with unshrivelled stalks.
Defects Fruits that are small, unripe or overripe, of dull colour or that are splitting or have any blemish or that lack stalks or have shrivelled stalks.
Advice to judges Handle the fruit carefully, by the stalk.

Condition	3 points
Uniformity	3 points
Size	3 points
Colour	3 points
TOTAL	12 points

Cherries, sweet
Merits Large, ripe fruits, of brilliant colour, with unshrivelled stalks.
Defects Fruits that are small, unripe or overripe, of dull colour or that are splitting or have any blemish or that lack stalks or have shrivelled stalks.
Advice to judges Handle the fruit carefully, by the stalk.

Condition	4 points
Uniformity	4 points
Size	4 points
Colour	4 points
TOTAL	16 points

Chuckleberries
See *Worcesterberries and currant × gooseberry hybrids*, p80.

Judging fruits

Citrus fruits
Merits Large, shapely, ripe fruits of good even colour natural to the cultivar, with bright, shiny, unblemished skins.
Defects Fruits that are small, misshapen, unripe or overripe, of dull or uneven colour or have any blemish.
Advice to judges Citrus fruit are shown without stalks.

Condition	5 points
Uniformity	5 points
Size	4 points
Colour	4 points
TOTAL	18 points

Currants, black
Merits Strigs with full complement of berries. Berries large, ripe and of a uniform, bright, jet-black colour. Stalks fresh.
Defects Strigs without full complement of berries. Berries small, unripe or overripe, or unevenly ripened, or of a dull colour or having shrivelled stalks.
Advice to judges Handle the fruit carefully, by the strig.

Condition	3 points
Uniformity	3 points
Size	3 points
Colour	3 points
TOTAL	12 points

Currants, other than black
Merits Strigs with full complement of berries. Berries large, ripe and of a uniform, brilliant colour. Stalks fresh.
Defects Strigs without full complement of berries. Berries small, unripe or overripe or unevenly ripened or of a dull colour or having shrivelled stalks.
Advice to judges Handle the fruit carefully, by the strig.

Condition	3 points
Uniformity	3 points
Size	3 points
Colour	3 points
TOTAL	12 points

Currant × gooseberry hybrids
See Worcesterberries and currant × gooseberry hybrids, p80.

Damsons and bullaces

All damsons and bullaces rank as cooking fruits.

Merits Large, ripe but firm fruits, of good colour, carrying perfect bloom and having stalks.

Defects Fruits small, unripe or so ripe as to be soft, of poor colour or with imperfect bloom or lacking stalks.

Advice to judges Handle the fruits carefully by the stalk to avoid damaging the bloom.

Condition	2 points
Uniformity	2 points
Size	2 points
Colour	2 points
TOTAL	8 points

Figs

Merits Large, fully ripe fruits, of good colour with bloom and stalks intact.

Defects Fruits small, unripe, of poor colour or with imperfect bloom.

Advice to judges Slight splitting is not a defect in ripe fruits. Handle the fruits very carefully.

Condition	5 points
Uniformity	3 points
Size	5 points
Colour	3 points
TOTAL	16 points

Gages

See Plums, dessert, and gages, p78.

Gooseberries

Merits Large, ripe or unripe fruits as appropriate for the season, uniform and unblemished, of good colour, complete with stalks.

Defects Fruits small, uneven, overripe, diseased, blemished, of poor colour or lacking stalks.

Advice to judges Check for fruits splitting and the presence of stalks.

Condition	4 points
Uniformity	3 points
Size	3 points
Colour	2 points
TOTAL	12 points

Judging fruits

Grapes, glasshouse dessert

Merits Large complete bunches, although large bunches of a poor quality are not so meritorious as smaller ones of a good quality. Symmetrical, complete, well-balanced bunches, of uniform size and shape and properly thinned so that each berry has had room to develop. Large berries, of uniform size, good colour, fully ripe and well finished with a dense, intact bloom.

Defects Bunches that are small, ill balanced, lacking uniformity in size or shape or that are loose or so crowded that some berries have not had room to develop properly. Berries that are small, lacking in uniformity, of poor colour or not fully ripe and poorly finished or overripe, diseased or that have little or only imperfect bloom or have withered stems or have spots or blemishes of any sort.

Advice to judges The fruit should be shown with a piece of lateral shoot on either side of the stalk to form a T-handle. The bunches should be shown on a stand unless another form of staging is allowed.

Condition	5 points
Size, shape and density of bunch	5 points
Size and uniformity of berry	5 points
Colour	5 points
TOTAL	20 points

Grapes, grown outdoors for wine or dessert

Merits Large, complete, well-filled and balanced bunches carrying large berries, unblemished, typical of the cultivar, of uniform size, good colour, fully ripe and well finished with a dense, intact bloom.

Defects Bunches that are small, underdeveloped or lacking uniformity. Berries that are blemished, rotting, split, have withered stems, unripe or overripe, poorly finished or with little or imperfect bloom.

Advice to judges Fruit should be cut from the vine with approximately 50mm of stalk.

Condition	4 points
Size and uniformity of berry	4 points
Size, shape and density of bunch	4 points
Colour	4 points
TOTAL	16 points

Huckleberries
See Other fruits, p80.

Japanese loquats
See Other fruits, p80.

Japanese wineberries
See Blackberries and hybrid cane fruits, p69.

Jostaberries
See **Worcesterberries and currant × gooseberry hybrids**, p80.

Kiwanos
See **Melons, horned**.

Kiwi fruits (Chinese gooseberries)
Merits   Large, ripe fruits, evenly shaped and uniform, with unblemished skins and stalks intact.
Defects   Fruits that are small, unripe or are uneven, lack uniformity or have any blemish or are without stalks.
Advice to judges   Check for ripeness.

Condition	4 points
Uniformity	4 points
Size	4 points
TOTAL	12 points

Loganberries
See **Blackberries and hybrid cane fruits**, p69.

Medlars
Merits   Fruits that have clean skins, stalks intact, size according to cultivar.
Defects   Fruits that are firm, small for the cultivar or have blotched skins.
Advice to judges   Can be shown either ripe or unripe, but ripe fruits are to be preferred. Ensure that fruits are not overripe, splitting or rotting.

Condition	3 points
Uniformity	3 points
Size	2 points
TOTAL	8 points

Melons
Merits   Large fruit (for the cultivar), clean, shapely, free from blemishes, fully ripe and well finished.
Defects   Small fruit (for the cultivar), or one that is unripe or overripe or is blemished or misshapen.
Advice to judges   Gently press the skin of a melon, which should 'give' a little when ripe, and there should be a slight aroma. Melons should be cut from the vine with approximately 50mm of stalk.

Condition	6 points
Size	6 points
Colour and finish	6 points
TOTAL	18 points

Melons, horned (kiwanos)

Merits Large, ripe fruits, clean, firm, of uniform golden or orange colour; blemish-free and well finished.
Defects Small, unripe fruits, damaged or of poor colour, lacking firmness, or overripe.
Advice to judges Melons should be cut from the vine with approximately 50mm of stalk.

Condition	4 points
Size	4 points
Colour and finish	4 points
TOTAL	12 points

Mulberries

Merits Large, ripe fruits of good colour, free from blemishes and in excellent condition.
Defects Fruits that are small, unripe or overripe, of a dull colour, not in good condition, imperfectly formed or have blemishes.
Advice to judges Handle the fruits carefully.

Condition	2 points
Uniformity	2 points
Size	2 points
Colour	2 points
TOTAL	8 points

Nectarines

*See **Peaches and nectarines**, p76.*

Nuts

Merits Large nuts with clean shells and plump kernels filling the cavities. In walnuts, nuts that are well sealed with thin shells.
Defects Nuts that are small, or have spotted shells, shrivelled or no kernels, or kernels that do not fill the shells or are unsound. In walnuts, nuts that are poorly sealed or have shells that are not thin.
Advice to judges Nuts are shown without stalks or husks. At least one specimen from each exhibit should be opened to ensure the kernel is full.

Condition	4 points
Uniformity	4 points
Size	4 points
TOTAL	12 points

Passion fruits

*See **Other fruits**, p80.*

Peaches and nectarines

Merits Large fruits (for the cultivar), fully ripe with the colour natural to the cultivar well developed, free from bruises and other blemishes.

Defects Fruits that are small (for the cultivar), unripe or overripe with colour not well developed, or bruised or with any other blemish.

Advice to judges For show purposes, peaches and nectarines are shown without stalks. Handle the fruits carefully to avoid bruising.

Condition	5 points
Uniformity	5 points
Size	5 points
Colour	5 points
TOTAL	20 points

Pears, Asian

Merits Large, shapely fruits with undamaged eyes, stalks intact, of good colour and with unblemished clear or finely russeted skins characteristic of the cultivar.

Defects Fruits that are small, misshapen or shrivelled, or lack stalks or of poor colour or have any blemish.

Advice to judges Ensure that all stalks are present.

Condition	6 points
Uniformity	6 points
Size	4 points
Colour	4 points
TOTAL	20 points

Pears, cooking

Merits Large (for the cultivar), shapely fruits with undamaged eyes, stalks intact and clear, unblemished skins of a colour characteristic of the cultivar.

Defects Fruits that are small for the cultivar, misshapen, overripe or soft or that have damaged eyes or lack stalks or have any blemish.

Advice to judges Only those pears listed as cooking pears (see p85) can be accepted as cooking pears. Ensure that all stalks are present.

Condition	6 points
Uniformity	6 points
Size	6 points
TOTAL	18 points

Pears, dessert

Merits Large for the cultivar, shapely fruits with undamaged eyes, stalks intact and clear, unblemished skins of the natural colour characteristic of the cultivar.

Defects Fruits that are small, misshapen or shrivelled or that have damaged eyes or lack stalks or are not well-coloured or have any blemish.

Advice to judges Check each fruit for over ripeness and the presence of a stalk.

Condition	6 points
Uniformity	6 points
Size	4 points
Colour	4 points
TOTAL	20 points

Persimmons

See Other fruits, p80.

Pineapple guavas

See Other fruits, p80.

Pineapples

Merits A fruit that is large for the cultivar, ripe and of a golden colour throughout, shapely, with segments of even size, free from blemish and having a fresh-looking crown that is in proportion to the fruit, ie about half its length.

Defects A fruit that is small for the cultivar, not fully ripe or overripe, of uneven shape, having poorly formed segments due to imperfect fertilisation, showing pest damage, having a crown that is not fresh or is not in proportion to the fruit.

Advice to judges Check the fruit carefully for overripe segments.

Condition	10 points
Size	6 points
Colour	4 points
TOTAL	20 points

Plums, cooking

Merits Large, firm, ripe fruits, of good colour, carrying perfect bloom, and having stalks.

Defects Fruits that are small, unripe or so ripe as to be soft, of poor colour or with imperfect bloom or lacking stalks.

Advice to judges Handle the fruit carefully, by the stalk to avoid damaging the bloom.

Condition	4 points
Uniformity	3 points
Size	4 points
Colour	3 points
TOTAL	14 points

Plums, dessert, and gages

Merits Large, fully ripe fruits, of good colour, with bloom intact and having stalks.

Defects Fruits that are small, unripe or overripe, of poor colour, with imperfect bloom or lacking stalks.

Advice to judges Handle the fruit carefully, by the stalk to avoid damaging the bloom. Slight shrivelling in gages is not a defect.

Condition	5 points
Uniformity	4 points
Size	3 points
Colour	4 points
TOTAL	16 points

Pluots

Judged to the same standards as *Plums, dessert, and gages*, above.

Quinces

Merits Large, shapely fruits with eyes and stalks intact and unblemished skins.

Defects Fruits that are small or misshapen or have damaged eyes or lack stalks or have any blemish.

Advice to judges Check carefully for any rots forming around the stalk.

Condition	4 points
Uniformity	4 points
Size	4 points
TOTAL	12 points

Raspberries

Merits Large, ripe fruits, of good colour, free from blemishes, in good condition, with fresh calyces, and having stalks.
Defects Fruits that are small, unripe or overripe, of a dull colour, not in good condition or have blemishes due to pest damage or imperfect fertilisation, or that lack stalks.
Advice to judges Handle the fruit carefully, by the stalk to avoid damaging the fruits.

Condition	4 points
Uniformity	2 points
Size	3 points
Colour	3 points
TOTAL	12 points

Strawberries

Merits Large, ripe fruits, of good colour, bright and fresh, free from blemish, in good condition, with fresh calyces, and having stalks.
Defects Fruits that are small, unripe or overripe, of a dull colour, not in good condition or that are "hard-nosed" through imperfect fertilisation, or lacking stalks.
Advice to judges Handle the fruit carefully, by the stalk to avoid bruising the fruits.

Condition	4 points
Uniformity	4 points
Size	4 points
Colour	4 points
TOTAL	16 points

Strawberries, alpine
See *Other fruits*, p80.

Sylvanberries
See *Blackberries and hybrid cane fruits*, p69.

Tamarillos or tree tomatoes
See *Other fruits*, p80.

Tayberries
See *Blackberries and hybrid cane fruits*, p69.

Worcesterberries and currant × gooseberry hybrids
eg jostaberries, and chuckleberries

Merits   Strigs with full complement of berries. Berries large, ripe, uniform and of even colour. Stalks fresh.

Defects   Strigs without full complement of berries. Berries small, unripe or overripe, of poor or uneven colour, diseased or blemished or having shrivelled stalks.

Advice to judges   Handle the fruit carefully, by the strig.

Condition	3 points
Uniformity	3 points
Size	3 points
Colour	3 points
TOTAL	12 points

Other fruits

This is a category to cover fruits not usually seen on the show bench but which may occur from time to time. Fruits currently in this category are listed below, each with a recommended points value. Where not given in the table (*see* pp66–67), the number of specimens for larger fruits should be at least 5, and 10 for smaller fruits. The considerations of condition, uniformity, size and colour will apply in equal measures.

Chokeberries (*Aronia melanocarpa*)	8 points
Fuchsia species (edible cultivars)	8 points
Garden huckleberries (*Solanum scabrum*)	8 points
Goji berries (*Lycium barbarum* and *L. chinense*)	12 points
Honeyberries (*Lonicera caerulea*)	12 points
Huckleberries (*Gaylussacia baccata*)	8 points
Japanese loquats (*Eriobotrya japonica*)	10 points
Melon pears or pepino dulce (*Solanum muricatum*)	12 points
Passion fruits (*Passiflora* species)	12 points
Persimmons (*Diospyros kaki*)	12 points
Pineapple guavas (*Acca sellowiana*)	10 points
Saskatoon berries (*Amelanchier alnifolia*)	10 points
Strawberries, alpine (*Fragaria vesca*)	8 points
Strawberry tree fruit (*Arbutus unedo*)	10 points
Tamarillo or tree tomatoes (*Solanum betaceum*)	12 points

Classified list of fruits

For exhibition purposes it is necessary to distinguish between dessert and cooking cultivars of apples, pears and plums; the following lists are drawn up for this purpose alone. Fruits such as these must be exhibited as dessert or cooking cultivars in accordance with these lists. The apples denoted as either small or large are classified as dual-purpose fruits (see *Dual-purpose cultivars*, p65).

Asterisks (*) indicate russet cultivars of dessert apples.

Apples, dessert

'Acme'
'Adams's Pearmain'
'Alkmeme' (Early Windsor)
'Allen's Everlasting'*
'Allington Pippin'
Ambassy ('Dalil')
'Ard Cairn Russet'*
'Aromatic Russet'*
'Ashmead's Kernel'*
'Autento'
'Autumn Pearmain'
'Baker's Delicious'
'Bardsey'
'Barnack Beauty'
'Barnack Orange'
'Baumann's Reinette'
'Baya Marisa' (Tickled Pink)
'Beauty of Bath'
'Beauty of Hants', **small fruits**
'Bella Bionda Patrizia'
'Belle de Boskoop', **small fruits**
'Ben's Red'
'Bess Pool'
'Blenheim Orange', **small fruits**
'Bloody Ploughman'
'Blue Moon'
Bolero ('Tuscan')
'Boston Russet', see
   'Roxbury Russet'
'Braddick's Nonpareil'
'Braeburn'
'Brownlee's Russet'*
'Calville Blanc d'Hiver'
'Calville Rouge Précocé', see
   'Reinette Rouge Etoilée'
'Captain Kidd'
'Charles Ross', **small fruits**
'Cheddar Cross'
'Cherry Cox'
'Chivers' Delight'
'Christmas Pearmain'
'Christmas Pippin'
'Claygate Pearmain'
'Cobra', **small fruits**
'Cockle Pippin'*
'Colonel Vaughan'
   (syn. 'Kentish Pippin')
'Cornish Aromatic'
'Cornish Gilliflower'
'Coronation'
'Court Pendu Plat'
'Cox's Orange Pippin'
'Crimson Cox'
Crispin ('Mutsu'), **small fruits**
'Crowngold'
'Cutler Grieve'
Cybèle ('Delrouval')
'D'Arcy Spice'*
Delbards ('Jubilee')
Delbarestivale ('Delcorf')
'Delblush' (Tentation)
'Delcorf' (Delbarestivale)
'Delfloki'
'Delkistar' (Regali)
'Delicious'
'Detardive'
'Delrouval' (Cybèle)
'Devonshire Quarrenden'
'Discovery'
'Duchess's Favourite'
'Duke of Devonshire'*
Early Windsor ('Alkmene')

Apples, dessert (continued)
'Egremont Russet'*
'Ellison's Orange'
'Elstar'
'Empire'
'Exeter Cross'
'Falstaff'
'Fearn's Pippin'
'Fiesta' (Red Pippin)
'Firedance'
Flamenco ('Obelisk')
'Fuji'
'Gala'
'Garden Fountain'
'Garden Sun Red'
'Gascoyne's Scarlet', **small fruits**
'Gavin'
'George Carpenter'
'George Cave'
'Gladstone'
'Gloster 69'
'Golden Delicious'
'Golden Gate'
'Golden Reinette'
'Golden Russet'*
'Goldrush'
'Granny Smith'
'Gravenstein'
'Greenfinch'
'Greensleeves'
'Herefordshire Russet'*
'Herring's Pippin', **small fruits**
'Holstein'
'Hubbard's Pearmain'
'Idared'
'Ingrid Marie'
'Irish Peach'
'James Grieve'
'Jerseymac'
'Jester'
'John Standish'
'Jonagold'
'Jonagored'
'Jonathan'
'Jubilee' (Delbards)
'Jumbo', **small fruits**
'Jupiter'
'Jupp's Russet'*
'Karmijn de Sonnaville'
'Katja' (Katy)
'Kent'
'Kentish Pippin', see
    'Colonel Vaughan'
'Kerry Pippin'
'Kidd's Orange Red'
'King of the Pippins'
'King Russet'*
'King's Acre Pippin'*
'Lady Sudeley'
'Langley Pippin'
'Laxton's Early Crimson'
'Laxton's Epicure'
'Laxton's Fortune'
'Laxton's Pearmain'
'Laxton's Superb'
'Limelight'
'Little Pax'
'Lord Burghley'
'Lord Hindlip'
'Lord Lambourne'
'Mabbott's Pearmain'
'McIntosh Red'
'Madresfield Court'
'Mannington's Pearmain'
'Margil'
'May Queen'
'Melba'
'Meridian'
'Melrose'
'Merton Beauty'
'Merton Knave'
'Merton Prolific'
'Merton Russet'*
'Merton Worcester'
'Michaelmas Red'
'Miller's Seedling'
'Millicent Barnes'
'Mother'
'Mutsu' (Crispin), **small fruits**
'Nanny'
'Newtown Pippin'
'Nonpareil'*
'Norfolk Royal'
'Norfolk Royal Russet'*

Judging fruits

'Nutmeg Pippin'*
'Obelisk' (Flamenco)
'Orleans Reinette'
'Paroquet'
'Pearl'
'Pine Golden Pippin'*
'Pineapple Russet'*
'Pinova'
'Pitmaston Russet Nonpareil'*
'Pitmaston Pine Apple'
'Pixie'
Polka ('Trajan')
'Queen Cox'
'Rajka'
'Red Delicious'
'Red Devil'
'Red Ellison'
'Red Juneating'
'Red Melba'
Red Pippin ('Fiesta')
'Red Pixie'
'Redlove Era'
'Redlove Sirena'
'Redsleeves'
Regali ('Delkistar')
'Reinette du Canada'*
'Reinette Rouge Etoilée'
  (syn. 'Calville Rouge Précoce')
'Ribston Pippin'
'Rival'
'Rosemary Russet'*
'Ross Nonpareil'
'Roundway Magnum Bonum', **small fruits**
'Roxbury Russet'
  (syn. 'Boston Russet')*
Royal Gala ('Tenroy')
'Rubinette'
'Saint Cecilia'
'Saint Edmund's Pippin'*
  (syn. 'Saint Edmund's Russet')
'Saint Everard'
'Saltcote Pippin'
'Santana'
'Sanspareil'
'Saturn'
'Scarlet Nonpareil'
'Scrumptious'
'Sir John Thornycroft'
'Smoothee'
'Spartan'
'Stark's Earliest'
'Star of Devon'
'Sturmer Pippin'
'Summerred'
'Sunrise'
'Sunset'
'Suntan'
'Sweet Society'
'Telamon' (Waltz)
'Tenroy' (Royal Gala)
Tentation ('Delblush')
Tickled Pink ('Baya Marisa')
'Topaz'
'Trajan' (Polka)
'Tydeman's Early Worcester'
'Tydeman's Late Orange'
'Vistabella'
'Wagener'
Waltz ('Telamon')
'Wealthy'
'White Joeneting'
'White Transparent'
'William Crump'
'Winston'
'Winter Banana'
'Winter Gem'
'Winter Queening'
'Woolbrook Pippin'
'Worcester Pearmain'
'Wyken Pippin'*
'Yellow Ingestrie'
'Zabergau Reinette'*

Apples, cooking

'Arthur W. Barnes'
'Alfriston'
'Annie Elizabeth'
'Arthur Turner'
'Beauty of Hants', **large fruits**
'Beauty of Kent'
'Belle de Boskoop', **large fruits**
'Belle de Pontoise'
'Bess Pool'
'Bismarck'
'Blenheim Orange', **large fruits**
'Bountiful'
'Bow Hill Pippin'
'Bramley's Seedling'
'Broadholm Beauty'
'Bushey Grove'
'Burr Knot'
'Carlisle Codlin'
'Catshead'
'Cellini'
'Charles Ross', **large fruits**
'Charlotte'
'Chelmsford Wonder'
'Cobra', **large fruits**
'Cottenham Seedling'
'Cox's Pomona'
'Crawley Beauty'
'Crimson Bramley'
'Crimson Peasgood'
Crispin ('Mutsu'), **large fruits**
'Don's Delight'
'Duchess of Oldenburg'
'Dummellor's Seedling'
  (syns. 'Dumelow's Seedling',
  'Wellington',
  'Normanton Wonder')
'Early Victoria', see 'Emneth Early'
'Ecklinville'
'Edward VII'
'Emneth Early' (syn 'Early
  Victoria')
'Encore'
'French Crab'
'Galloway Pippin'
'Gascoyne's Scarlet', **large fruits**
'George Neal'
'Gloria Mundi'
'Golden Noble'
'Golden Spire'
'Gooseberry'
'Grenadier'
'Hambledon Deux Ans'
'Harvey'
'Hawthornden'
'Herefordshire Beefing'
'Herring's Pippin', **large fruits**
'Hoary Morning'
'Howgate Wonder'
'Jumbo', **large fruits**
'Keswick Codlin'
'Lady Henniker'
'Lane's Prince Albert'
'Lemon Pippin'
'Lodi'
'Lord Derby'
'Lord Grosvenor'
'Lord Stradbroke'
'Lord Suffield'
'Mere de Menage'
'Monarch'
'Mutsu' (Crispin), **large fruits**
'Nancy Jackson'
'Newton Wonder'
'Norfolk Beauty'
'Norfolk Beefing'
'Northern Greening'
'Normanton Wonder', see
  'Dummellor's Seedling'
'Peasgood's Nonsuch'
'Queen'
'Red Victoria'
'Reverend W. Wilks'
'Roundway Magnum
  Bonum', **large fruits**
'Royal Jubilee'
'Royal Russet'
'Sandringham'
'Stirling Castle'
'Striped Beefing'
'Tom Putt'
'Tower of Glamis'
'Upton Pyne'

'Warner's King'
'Wellington', see
'Dummellor's Seedling'
'Woolbrook Russet'*

Damsons, including bullaces

All damsons and bullaces rank as cooking fruits.

Pears

The following are classified as cooking pears at RHS shows:
'Bellissime d'Hiver'
'Beurré Claigeau'
'Black Worcester'
'Catillac'
'Uvedale's St Germain'
'Vicar of Winkfield'

Plums, dessert

'Allgroves Superb'
'Angelina Burdett'
'Anita'
'Anna Spath'
'Ariel'
'Avalon'
'Blue Rock'
'Blue Tit'
'Bonne de Bry'
'Bryanston Gage'
'Burbank's Tangerine'
'Coe's Golden Drop'
'Count Althann's Gage'
'Cox's Emperor'
'Crimson Drop'
'Denniston's Superb', see 'Imperial Gage'
'Early Rivers' (syn. 'Early Prolific')
'Edda'
'Excalibur'
gages: all cultivars
'Golden Globe'
'Golden Sphere'
'Goldfinch'
'Grove's Late Victoria'
'Guinevere'
'Gypsy'
'Haganta'
'Herman'
'Imperial Gage' (syn. 'Denniston's Superb')
'Jefferson'
'Jojo'
'Jubilaeum'
'Kirke's'
'Lancelot'
'Laxton's Delicious'
'Laxton's Gage'
'Lizzie'
'Mann's No 1'
'Meritaire'
'Merton Gem'
'Miraclaude'
'Ontario'
'Opal'
'Oullin's Gage'
'Reeves Seedling'
'Reine-Claude Dorée'
'Reine-Claude Vraie'
'Sanctus Hubertus'
'Seneca'
'Severn Cross'
'Thames Cross'
'Utility'
'Valerie'
'Valor'
'Verity'
'Victoria'
'Victory'
'Violetta'
'Washington'

Plums, cooking
'Belgian Purple'
'Belle de Louvain'
'Blaisdon Red'
'Curlew'
'Czar'
'Diamond'
'Early Laxton'
'Edwards'
'Giant Prune'
'Guinevere'
'Heron'
'Laxton's Cropper'
'Marjorie's Seedling'
mirabelles: all cultivars
'Monarch'
'Myrobalan'
'Pershore'
'Pond's Seedling'
'President'
'Purple Pershore'
'Warwickshire Drooper'
'White Magnum Bonum'

Judging fruits

JUDGING VEGETABLES

In assessing the merits of exhibits of vegetables the following features should be considered: condition, uniformity, size and colour.

A dish must consist of one cultivar only.

Condition   All vegetables should be clean, fresh, tender and free of coarseness and blemishes.

Uniformity   All the specimens exhibited on a dish should be alike in size, shape, condition and colour. When only one specimen is shown and points for uniformity are available, those points should be excluded.

Size   Large specimens are preferable but only if they are of good quality as the production of large specimens of good quality requires more skill than the production of small specimens.

Colour   Colour should be fresh and true to the cultivar at maturity. There are now many vegetables available in a range of colours. Good colour for the cultivar should be the main consideration.

Constitution of dishes

Unless otherwise specified it is suggested that the numbers given in the table below are used for larger shows. Smaller shows should adopt smaller quantities, half the quantity stated (rounded up), and no less than two, being the recommended minimum unless only one is required for larger shows.

Maximum points for a dish   The exhibition value of points available depends on the difficulty of producing a perfect dish (*seeRule 7, p60*). The maximum points for a dish are as follows:

	Number of specimens required for single dishes of vegetables	Maximum points for a dish
Artichokes, Chinese	9	12
Artichokes, globe	2	15
Artichokes, Jerusalem	6	10
Asparagus	6	15
Asparagus peas	12 pods	12
Aubergines	3	18

Judging vegetables

	Number	Points
Aubergines	3	18
Beans, broad, French, climbing or dwarf	9 pods	15
Beans, runner	9 pods	18
Beans, shelling, other than broad *eg* borlotti types and similar	9 pods	15
Beetroot, cylindrical, globe	4	15
Beetroot, long	3	20
Broccoli, sprouting (shoots)	12	15
Brussels sprouts	15	15
Cabbages, Chinese, green, red, Savoy	2	15
Calabrese (heads*)	2	15
Carrots, long pointed	3	20
Carrots, stump rooted	3	18
Cauliflowers	2	20
Celeriac	2	15
Celery, blanched or trench	2	20
Celery, self-blanching or green	2	18
Chicory, chicons, radicchio and other forced heads	3	15
Chives	1 bunch **	10
Corn salad (lambs' lettuce)	1 bunch of 9 plants	10
Courgettes	3	12
Cress (seedlings)	***	10
Cress, American or land	1 bunch of 9 plants	10
Cucumbers, grown under protection	2	18
Cucumbers, outdoor grown	2	15
Cucumbers, mini or small; gherkins and pickling types	6	15
Endive, all types	2	15

	Number	Points
Fennel, Florence	2	15
Flower sprout, Petit Posy and similar	15	15
Garlic, elephant or giant	3 bulbs	15
Garlic	5 bulbs	12
Herbs, culinary	1 bunch **	12
Herbs, culinary growing in pots	1 pot	12
Kale (leaves)	10	12
Kohlrabi	3	12
Leeks, blanched or intermediate	3	20
Leeks, pot	2	20
Lettuces, butterhead, cos	2	15
Lettuce, loose-leaf	2 heads	12
Marrows	2	15
Mushrooms	12	15
Mustard or rape (seedlings)	***	10
Okra	3	18
Onions, large exhibition	3	20
Onions, 250g or under	5	15
Onions, green salad or spring	12	12
Onions, on ropes	plait of 8	20
Onions, pickling	12	12
Oriental brassicas (flowering stalks)	12	15
Oriental brassicas (heading types)	2	15
Oriental brassicas (loose-leaved types)	2	12
Parsnips	3	20
Peas	9 pods	20
Peas, mangetout or snap	9 pods	15

Judging vegetables

	Number	Points
Peppers, hot (chilli)	6	15
Peppers, sweet	3	15
Potatoes	5	20
Pumpkins	1	10
Radishes, Oriental, winter	3	15
Radishes, small salad	9	12
Rhubarb, forced	3 sticks	15
Rhubarb, natural	3 sticks	12
Salad vegetables, miscellaneous	2	10
Salsify and scorzonera	2	15
Seakale (heads)	2	15
Shallots, large exhibiton	12	18
Shallots, pickling	12	15
Spinach, spinach beet or chard	15 leaves	12
Spinach, New Zealand	15 tips	12
Squash, summer	3	12
Squash, winter	1	10
Swedes	2	15
Sweet corn	3	18
Tomatoes, large	3	15
Tomatoes, medium	9	18
Tomatoes, small	15	12
Tomatoes, truss	1	15
Turnips	3	15
Watercress	1 bunch **	10

* Calabrese sideshoots should be exhibited as broccoli, sprouting.

** Chives, watercress or any herb should be sufficient to fill a vase approximately 150mm high and 65mm at the mouth.

*** Mustard and cress should be exhibited in growth, not cut and be shown in not less than two 150mm pans or their equivalent. If both mustard and cress are shown they will count as one item. Either may be shown alone. Rape will count as mustard.

Alphabetical list of vegetables

Artichokes, Chinese
Merits Well shaped, clean rhizomes, around 40mm long with unblemished skins.
Defects Small or oversized tubers, irregularly shaped or damaged.
Advice to judges Look for tubers that are clean, well-shaped and of appropriate size.

Condition	4 points
Uniformity	3 points
Size	2 points
Shape	3 points
TOTAL	12 points

Artichokes, globe
Merits Large, heavy, shapely, well-closed heads of plump, solid fleshy scales.
Defects Heads that are small, lightweight, irregular or loose, or that have thin or shrivelled scales.
Advice to judges Look for well-grown specimens with symmetrical heads and closely-knit scales.

Condition	5 points
Uniformity	3 points
Size	2 points
Shape	2 points
Colour	3 points
TOTAL	15 points

Artichokes, Jerusalem
Merits Shapely, large rhizomes with smooth, unblemished skins.
Defects Small or oversized rhizomes, irregularly shaped, damaged with rough or patchy skins.

Condition	4 points
Uniformity	2 points
Size	2 points
Shape	2 points
TOTAL	10 points

Judging vegetables

Asparagus
Merits Fresh, long, straight, plump, dark green stems with well-closed scales.
Defects Stems that are not fresh, or are short, crooked, thin, shrivelled or dull-coloured, or that have open scales.

Condition	5 points
Uniformity	3 points
Size	3 points
Shape	2 points
Colour	2 points
TOTAL	15 points

Asparagus peas
Merits Well-shaped tender unblemished pods, approximately 20–30mm long with stalks attached.
Defects Misshapen, damaged pods that are tough or immature or that lack stalks.

Condition	4 points
Uniformity	3 points
Size of pods	3 points
Colour	2 points
TOTAL	12 points

Aubergines
Merits Large, shapely, solid, bright, well-coloured fruits free from blemishes and with fresh calyces.
Defects Fruits that are small, misshapen, shrivelled, dull or poorly coloured.
Advice to judges Fruits should be firm and of good shape with natural bloom and fresh calyces.

Condition	5 points
Uniformity	4 points
Size	3 points
Shape	3 points
Colour	3 points
TOTAL	18 points

Beans, broad

Merits Fresh, well-filled pods with stalks and clear unblemished skins and tender seeds of good size.
Defects Not fresh or that are blemished, imperfectly filled or contain seeds that are not tender.
Advice to judges Choose long, blemish-free pods. Open one pod from each exhibit. Seeds should not have dark hilums ('eyes'), be split, be detached from the pod or show evidence of pest or disease damage.

Condition	5 points
Uniformity	3 points
Size	3 points
Shape	2 points
Colour	2 points
TOTAL	15 points

Beans, French, climbing or dwarf

Merits Straight, fresh, tender, pods with stalks, of good colour with no outward sign of seeds, of good size, even length and having uniform tails.
Defects Pods that are misshapen, dull, pale, shrivelled, tough, stringy or that have prominent seeds.
Advice to judges Snap one pod from each exhibit to determine freshness and condition.

Condition	5 points
Uniformity	3 points
Size	3 points
Shape	2 points
Colour	2 points
TOTAL	15 points

Beans, runner

Merits Long, uniform, straight, shapely, fresh pods of good colour with stalks and no outward sign of seeds.
Defects Pods that are short, misshapen, with rough skin, damaged or bottle-necked and when snapped are stringy, limp or show prominent seeds.
Advice to judges Snap one pod from each exhibit to determine freshness and condition.

Condition	5 points
Uniformity	4 points
Size	3 points
Shape	4 points
Colour	2 points
TOTAL	18 points

Beans, shelling, other than broad (*eg* borlotti and similar types)

Merits   Uniform, fresh well filled pods with stalks and displaying colour according to cultivar. The seeds should be prominent, of an even size, mature but not dry and the pods well developed.

Defects   Small, blemished pods, unevenly matched, imperfectly filled and of poor colour or having dry pods with dry seeds.

Advice to judges   Open one pod from each exhibit to determine the condition of the bean and to ensure it is not immature or over mature.

Condition	5 points
Uniformity	3 points
Size	3 points
Shape	2 points
Colour	2 points
TOTAL	15 points

Beetroot, cylindrical

Merits   Well-proportioned, of approximately 150mm in length, with a single taproot and smooth skin of a uniform dark colour. Foliage trimmed to approximately 75mm.

Defects   Specimens that are too large, too small, misshapen, tough, multi-rooted, or are marked with pest or disease damage, have rough corky skin, or show signs of age.

Advice to judges   Look for specimens uniform in size, shape and colour with clean, firm, damage-free skin with a single taproot and foliage trimmed to approximately 75mm. It is not necessary to cut the exhibits to determine internal condition.

Condition	5 points
Uniformity	3 points
Size	2 points
Shape	3 points
Colour	2 points
TOTAL	15 points

Beetroot, globe

Merits Spherical, of approximately 60–75mm in diameter with a single taproot and smooth skin of a uniform colour. Foliage trimmed to approximately 75mm.
Defects Specimens that are too large, too small, misshapen, tough, multi-rooted, or are marked with pest or disease damage, have rough corky skin, or show signs of age.
Advice to judges Look for specimens uniform in size, shape and colour with clean, firm, damage-free skin with a single taproot and foliage trimmed to approximately 75mm. It is not necessary to cut the exhibits to determine internal condition.

Condition	5 points
Uniformity	3 points
Size	2 points
Shape	3 points
Colour	2 points
TOTAL	15 points

Beetroot, long

Merits Long, firm well-shaped roots, evenly tapered, with clean, broad shoulders, of a uniform colour and free from sideshoots. Foliage trimmed to approximately 75mm.
Defects Specimens that are misshapen, multi-rooted, rough, corky or corkscrewed, or that have cracked shoulders, or that feel spongy to the touch or are of poor colour.
Advice to judges Look for long, uniform, well-shaped roots with good, clean, firm, damage-free skins with a single taproot and foliage trimmed to approximately 75mm. It is not necessary to cut the exhibits to determine internal condition.

Condition	5 points
Uniformity	4 points
Size	4 points
Shape	4 points
Colour	3 points
TOTAL	20 points

Broccoli, sprouting

Merits Firm, fresh florets with tight heads with colour appropriate to the cultivar. Shown with approximately 75–100mm of stalk.
Defects Limp, blown, old florets with spongy texture and poor colour.

Condition	5 points
Uniformity	4 points
Size	3 points
Colour	3 points
TOTAL	15 points

Judging vegetables

Brussels sprouts
Merits Clean, fresh, solid, tightly closed buttons of good colour and free from blemishes.
Defects Sprouts that are old, loose-leaved, yellowing, excessively peeled, or that show signs of pest or disease damage.

Condition	5 points
Uniformity	4 points
Size	3 points
Colour	3 points
TOTAL	15 points

Cabbages, Chinese
Merits Fresh, firm, solid heads, outside leaves a fresh green colour, free from pest or disease damage, roots washed with approximately 75mm of stalk.
Defects Soft, loose heads that lack freshness, have too many outer leaves removed or are damaged by pests or disease.

Condition	5 points
Uniformity	5 points
Colour	5 points
TOTAL	15 points

Cabbages, green, red or Savoy
Merits Shapely, fresh and solid heads with the surrounding leaves free from any pest or disease damage with the bloom intact and of good colour. Shape according to cultivar with approximately 75mm of stalk.
Defects Heads that are soft, split, lack freshness, with the surrounding leaves showing damage due to pests or disease or have too many outer leaves removed.

Condition	5 points
Uniformity	3 points
Size	3 points
Shape	2 points
Colour	2 points
TOTAL	15 points

Calabrese, romanesco and other types (heads to be formed of immature, edible flowerheads)

Note: Calabrese sideshoots should be exhibited as Broccoli, sprouting
Merits Fresh, solid, tightly-closed heads of good colour.
Defects Heads that lack freshness or that are becoming loose, soft, flowering, or of poor colour, turning yellow.

Condition	5 points
Uniformity	3 points
Size	3 points
Shape	2 points
Colour	2 points
TOTAL	15 points

Capsicums

*See **Peppers, hot (chilli)** or **Peppers, sweet**, p117.*

Carrots, long-pointed

Long-pointed carrots have large, long taproots that can often reach one metre in length. The taproot gradually tapers over its length ending in a fine root.

Merits Fresh, firm, long, smooth roots of good shape, weight and colour maintained for the full length of the root. Skins clean and bright with no evidence of side roots. Foliage trimmed to approximately 75mm.
Defects Roots that are coarse, misshapen or split, have coloured crowns, are multi-rooted, dull, pale, poorly coloured, or that show evidence of pests, disease or of going to seed.

Condition	5 points
Uniformity	4 points
Size	4 points
Shape	3 points
Colour	4 points
TOTAL	20 points

Carrots, stump-rooted

Stump-rooted carrots have taproots which, when mature, develop a definite stump (blunt end). Chantenay types have broad-shouldered, straight, slightly tapered roots with a definite stump. Nantes types have medium-shouldered, cylindrical and straight roots with a definite stump.

Merits Fresh roots of good colour and shape with a decided stump. Skin clear and bright. Foliage trimmed to approximately 75mm.

Defects Roots that are coarse, misshapen or with coloured crowns; are multi-rooted, dull, pale or poorly coloured; showing evidence of pest or disease damage, ribbing, going to seed or lacking a decided stump.

Condition	5 points
Uniformity	4 points
Size	3 points
Shape	3 points
Colour	3 points
TOTAL	18 points

Cauliflowers, coloured

Merits Tight, solid, symmetrical heads of uniform, good colour, free from blemish, shown with approximately 75mm of stalk.

Defects Heads that are spongy, granular, significantly lumpy, or that are becoming loose around the edge. Curds that are of poor colour, showing leaf bracts, lacking uniformity, showing signs of pest or disease damage or that are underdeveloped, flat or not symmetrical.

Condition	5 points
Uniformity	4 points
Size	4 points
Shape	4 points
Colour	3 points
TOTAL	20 points

Cauliflowers, white

Merits Heads with symmetrical, close, solid, white curd, with smooth texture, free from blemish or stain, with approximately 75mm of stalk and foliage neatly trimmed. The curd should form a circle when viewed from above and have a medium-shaped dome when viewed from the side. The edges of the curds should be firm and close fitting.
Defects Heads that are spongy, granular, significantly lumpy, or that are becoming loose around the edge. Curds that are off-white, showing leaf bracts, lacking uniformity, showing signs of pest or disease damage or that are underdeveloped, flat or not symmetrical.

Condition	5 points
Uniformity	4 points
Size	4 points
Shape	4 points
Colour	3 points
TOTAL	20 points

Celeriac

Merits Blemish-free, globe-shaped roots. Foliage trimmed back to leave the central youngest leaves to approximately 75mm and roots trimmed back to the body of the vegetable.
Defects Roots that are rough, split or flat.
Advice to judges *See Merits and Defects, above*. Coloration around the root is not a defect.

Condition	5 points
Uniformity	4 points
Size	3 points
Shape	3 points
TOTAL	15 points

Celery, blanched or trench

Merits Large, well-blanched, firm, clean and crisp leaf stalks, free from blemish, pest or disease damage.

Defects Heads that are small, poorly blanched or showing evidence of pest damage. Leaf stalks that are thin, twisted, pithy, split, poorly blanched or showing sideshoots. Hearts that show evidence of rot or have visible flower stalk.

Advice to judges Remove all ties. Check the foliage for pest or disease damage. Examine the celery through 360 degrees noting blanch and arrangement of the stalks. Look inside the heart and check for heart rot, flower stalks, blistering and sideshoots between the leaf stalks. Finally, check that the root plate is not split and that the whole exhibit is clean, well-blanched and crisp.

Condition	5 points
Uniformity	4 points
Size	4 points
Shape	4 points
Colour	3 points
TOTAL	20 points

Celery, self-blanching or green

Merits Fresh, firm, crisp, with clean and blemish-free stalks and leaves. Self-blanching cultivars should be well blanched.

Defects Small, loose, thin, soft, pithy, or twisted stalks, with heart rot or visible flower stalks.

Advice to judges See *Celery, blanched or trench, above*.

Condition	5 points
Uniformity	4 points
Size	3 points
Shape	3 points
Colour	3 points
TOTAL	18 points

Chard

See Spinach, spinach beet or chard, p122.

Chicory, chicons, radicchio and other forced heads

Merits Large, solid, crisp, tender, well-formed, well-blanched heads with roots attached and colour according to cultivar.

Defects Chicons that are poorly developed, limp or blemished. Heads that are open, soft, loose, limp, tough or badly blanched.

Condition	5 points
Uniformity	3 points
Size	2 points
Shape	2 points
Colour	3 points
TOTAL	15 points

Chicory, sugarloaf type
See **Endive**, p106.

Chives
See **Salad vegetables, miscellaneous**, p127.

Corn salad or lambs' lettuce
See **Salad vegetables, miscellaneous**, p127.

Courgettes

Merits Young, tender fruits of good uniform shape and colour, approximately 150mm in length and approximately 25–35mm in diameter. Round cultivars should be approximately 75mm in diameter. Of any colour but well matched.

Defects Fruits that are not young or tender, or that are misshapen, ill-matched or showing evidence of pest or disease damage or disease.

Advice to judges Specimens may be shown with or without flowers attached.

Condition	4 points
Uniformity	3 points
Size	2 points
Shape	3 points
TOTAL	12 points

Cress
See **Salad vegetables, miscellaneous**, p127.

Cress, American or land
See **Salad vegetables, miscellaneous**, p127.

Cucumbers, grown under protection

Merits Fresh, young, green, tender, blemish-free, straight fruits, of uniform thickness with short handles.

Defects Fruits that are old, yellowing, crooked, soft, of irregular thickness, showing evidence of pest or disease damage, or are marked by the rubbing or contact with the stalks or leaves, or with long handles.

Advice to judges Specimens may be shown with or without flowers attached.

Condition	5 points
Uniformity	4 points
Size	3 points
Shape	3 points
Colour	3 points
TOTAL	18 points

Cucumbers, outdoor grown

For Merits, Defects and Advice to judges, see Cucumbers, grown under protection, above.

Condition	5 points
Uniformity	3 points
Size	2 points
Shape	2 points
Colour	3 points
TOTAL	15 points

Cucumbers, mini or small

Merits Fresh, young, green, tender, blemish-free, straight fruits approximately 100–200mm in length, matching in all respects and of uniform diameter.

Defects Fruits that are old, yellowing, crooked, soft, of irregular thickness, showing evidence of pest or disease damage, or are marked by the rubbing or contact with the stalks or leaves, or with long handles.

Advice to Judges Specimens may be shown with or without flowers attached. This is not a class for standard type cucumbers that have been poorly grown.

Condition	5 points
Uniformity	3 points
Size	2 points
Shape	2 points
Colour	3 points
TOTAL	15 points

Cucumbers, gherkins and pickling types

For Merits, Defects and Advice to judges, see Cucumbers, mini or small, p105.

Condition	5 points
Uniformity	3 points
Size	2 points
Shape	2 points
Colour	3 points
TOTAL	15 points

Endive and Chicory, sugarloaf type

Merits Fresh, well-shaped, solid heads, of good size with the outer leaves a fresh green colour. Free from pest and disease damage with roots attached.

Defects Small, limp heads, imperfectly blanched, blemished or that show evidence of pest or disease damage.

Condition	6 points
Uniformity	3 points
Size	2 points
Shape	2 points
Colour	2 points
TOTAL	15 points

Fennel

See Herbs, culinary p108.

Fennel, Florence

Merits Large, clean bulbs with fleshy, swollen leaf bases, free from coarseness or visible flower stems. Foliage trimmed back to approximately 75–100mm but with central, youngest foliage retained.

Defects Leaves that are small at the base, coarse or loose. Bulbs that are flat or elongated. Evidence of pest or disease damage.

Condition	4 points
Uniformity	3 points
Size	4 points
Shape	4 points
TOTAL	15 points

Flower sprout, Petit Posy

Merits Clean, fresh, uniform, well-coloured open sprouts, of medium size and free from blemishes.
Defects Old, overly large sprouts showing flower buds or elongated stalks or that show signs of pest or disease.

Condition	5 points
Uniformity	4 points
Size	3 points
Colour	3 points
TOTAL	15 points

Fruiting vegetables, miscellaneous

See *Fruiting vegetables, miscellaneous*, p126.

Garlic, elephant or giant

Merits Large, well-ripened bulbs. Specimens should be whole and not segmented; the white, outer papery skin should be intact and free of blemishes. Roots should be removed.
Defects Specimens that are split, displaying the segments and hard-shelled corms. Bulbs which are misshapen, immature or yellowing.
Advice to judges Check the neck and root plate for soundness. Bulbs should be displayed with approximately 75mm of dried stem.

Condition	5 points
Uniformity	3 points
Size	4 points
Colour	3 points
TOTAL	15 points

Garlic

Merits Well-shaped, solid, clean, well-ripened bulbs with thin necks, with dried stem of approximately 25mm.
Defects Bulbs that are misshapen, soft, poorly ripened or that have thick necks or broken skins.
Advice to judges When displayed for exhibition roots should be removed and bulbs must not be divided into segments (cloves).

Condition	5 points
Uniformity	3 points
Size	2 points
Colour	2 points
TOTAL	12 points

Gourds, edible

See *Squash, winter*, p123.

Gourds, ornamental

See p157 under *Judging Flowers and Ornamental Plants*.

Herbs, culinary

See Glossary, p189.
Merits Fresh, healthy, clean, blemish-free foliage.
Defects Material that is not fresh and clean, is yellowing or showing other signs of age or pest or disease damage, or has any disease.
Advice to judges Herbs exhibited within the vegetable section of a show should be for culinary purposes and therefore foliage is the predominant factor.

Condition	6 points
Size	3 points
Colour	3 points
TOTAL	12 points

Herbs, culinary growing in pots

See Glossary, p189.
Merits A sturdy, shapely plant, well furnished with clean, unblemished, healthy foliage. Size of the plant to be proportionate to the size of the pot.
Defects A drawn, undernourished plant with unhealthy, deformed, damaged or diseased foliage.
Advice to judges Herbs exhibited within the vegetable section of a show should be for culinary purposes and therefore foliage is the predominant factor.

Condition	6 points
Size	3 points
Colour	3 points
TOTAL	12 points

Kale

Note: see p46 on exhibiting in a vase.
Merits Fresh, well-developed, blemish-free leaves of good colour and size as per cultivar.
Defects Leaves that are limp, poorly developed, damaged or of poor colour.
Advice to judges Look for fresh clean specimens with well-developed leaves.

Condition	5 points
Uniformity	3 points
Size	2 points
Colour	2 points
TOTAL	12 points

Kohlrabi

Merits The swollen stems should be fresh, tender, round, retaining natural bloom, with small leaf bases and free from damage. Side foliage to be trimmed to approximately 20mm but with central, youngest foliage retained.

Defects Swollen stems that are misshapen, cracked or damaged, lacking natural bloom or have coarse leaf bases.

Condition	5 points
Uniformity	3 points
Size	2 points
Shape	2 points
TOTAL	12 points

Leaf vegetables, miscellaneous

See Leaf vegetables, miscellaneous, p126.

Leeks, blanched or intermediate

See note on p47 and Glossary, p190.

Merits Clean, firm, solid, parallel-sided, long barrels with no sign of softness or splits, with a tight button and free from bulbing and ribbiness. Foliage that is turgid and free from pest, disease or other damage.

Defects Leeks that are soft, thin, tapering, short-shafted, imperfectly blanched, discoloured or bulbous, or that have diseased or damaged leaves.

Advice to judges Specimens must be more than 150mm from root plate to button. Foliage should be dark green in colour, turgid, with no rust, pest damage or evidence of seeding. Barrels should be firm and sound with no sign of tapering or bulbing. Roots should be fresh with a sound root plate intact. Good specimens will have a long, distinct blanch that is in proportion to the circumference of the barrel. In close competition measuring the length and girth of each exhibit will aid selection.

Blanched leeks are more than 350mm in length; Intermediate leeks are between 150mm and 350mm in length. In small, local shows judges may consider leeks more than 150mm in length as blanched leeks. Roots must be washed but not trimmed.

Condition	6 points
Uniformity	4 points
Size	4 points
Shape	3 points
Colour	3 points
TOTAL	20 points

Leeks, pot

*See note on p47 and **Glossary**, p190.*

Merits Firm, solid, heavy, round leeks with unbroken, clean and unblemished skins. Fresh foliage that is free from pest, disease or other damage. Barrels that are parallel and well blanched with sound root plate and roots intact. Blanch must not be greater than 150mm from the root plate to the button.

Defects Leeks that are soft, thin, small, with a split button, shaft too long or ribby, evidence of seed-head. Barrels that taper or that are bulbous. Malformation or damage of any part including the root plate.

Advice to judges First check the length of the barrels. Specimens more than 150mm in length will be automatically disqualified. Foliage should be fresh, green, firm,damage-free and with no evidence of seeding. Barrels should be straight and well-blanched with a sound root plate and fresh roots. Roots must be washed but not trimmed. For guidance regarding size *see **Note**, below*.

Condition	6 points
Uniformity	4 points
Size	4 points
Shape	3 points
Colour	3 points
TOTAL	20 points

• Note: The National Pot Leek Society gives additional points for volume or cubic capacity measured on volume of blanched shaft to tight 150mm (6in) button (*ie* from basal plate to lowest unbroken leaf, including the veil where present and around the barrel). One point for every 164cm^3 (10in^3) and decimal point for part of 164cm^3 (10in^3). Tables for the calculation of cubic capacity are obtainable from the Secretary of the National Pot Leek Society.

Lettuces, butterhead

See note on p47 on exhibiting with roots.

Merits Fresh, clean, tender, unbroken, blemish-free heads of appropriate colour.

Defects Overtrimmed heads, limp, not clean, that show signs of bolting, showing signs of pest or disease damage, are blemished or are of poor colour. Roots not present.

Condition	6 points
Uniformity	4 points
Firmness and texture	3 points
Colour	2 points
TOTAL	15 points

Lettuces, cos

See note on p47 on exhibiting with roots.

Merits Crisp, fresh. Unbroken, blemish-free heads of good size and colour.

Defects Overtrimmed heads, limp, not clean, that show signs of bolting, showing signs of pest and disease damage, are blemished or are of poor colour. Roots not present.

Condition	6 points
Uniformity	4 points
Firmness and texture	3 points
Colour	2 points
TOTAL	15 points

Lettuces, crisp

See Lettuces, cos, above.

Lettuces, loose-leaf

See note on p47 on exhibiting with roots.

Merits Fresh, clean, tender, unbroken, blemish-free heads of appropriate colour.

Defects Overtrimmed heads, limp, not clean, that show signs of bolting, showing signs of pest and disease damage, are blemished or are of poor colour. Roots not present.

Condition	5 points
Uniformity	4 points
Colour	3 points
TOTAL	12 points

Marjoram

*See **Herbs**, culinary p108.*

Marrows

Merits Fresh, young fruits that should be less than 350mm in length or, in the case of round cultivars, approximately 500mm in circumference.

Defects Fruits that are not young or that are blemished, misshapen or ill-matched. Old and overripe marrows or fruits that exceed 350mm in length, or in the case of round-fruited cultivars, 500mm in circumference.

Advice to judges Downpoint specimens that are old, hard, or that are larger than the recommended sizes, or that are lacking uniformity. For guidance regarding size, *see **note**, p47*.

Condition	6 points
Uniformity	4 points
Size	3 points
Shape	2 points
TOTAL	15 points

Mint

*See **Herbs**, culinary p108.*

Mushrooms

Note Stage of development should be stated in the Schedule, ie "Button", "Closed Cap" or "Open Cap".
Merits Mushrooms that are well formed with unbroken edges and free from blemishes. If the gills are visible they should be pink in colour.
Defects Mushrooms that are blemished, misshapen, show any signs of shrivelling, are flattened, have broken edges or blackening gills.
Advice to judges Look for well-formed specimens with unbroken cap edges, free from blemish, with gills of a good colour where appropriate.

Condition	7 points
Uniformity	4 points
Colour	4 points
TOTAL	15 points

Mustard or rape

*See **Salad vegetables, miscellaneous**, p127.*

Okra

Merits Fresh, slender-pointed fruits, free from blemishes and less than 100mm long.
Defects Fruits that are misshapen, shrivelled, dull or poorly coloured, or more than 100mm long.
Advice to judges Downpoint fruits that are bulky, misshapen, old or poorly coloured, under- or oversized, or that lack uniformity.

Condition	6 points
Uniformity	5 points
Size	4 points
Colour	3 points
TOTAL	18 points

Onions, large exhibition

Merits Large firm, well-ripened bulbs with thin necks and unbroken skins, free from pest, disease or other damage. Sound and intact root plates.

Defects Bulbs that are small, misshapen, lopsided or blemished, or that have soft or thick necks, or indicate moisture present under the skin, or have broken outer skins or have unsound root plates.

Advice to judges Look for large, uniform, well-ripened bulbs, of good shape, free from any blemish, with roots trimmed and necks neatly tied with uncoloured raffia. At early summer shows or small local shows bulbs may be shown with tops trimmed, bulbs either dressed or as grown with roots washed.

Condition	6 points
Uniformity	4 points
Size	5 points
Shape	3 points
Colour	2 points
TOTAL	20 points

Onions, 250g or under

Merits Firm, thin-necked, blemish-free bulbs grown from either seed or sets with well-ripened, unbroken skins free from pest, disease or other damage.

Defects Bulbs that are too small or in excess of 250g, thick-necked, misshapen, blemished, or that have broken skins or have been skinned excessively.

Advice to judges All specimens must be weighed and any more than 250g must be disqualified. Bulbs should be as near to 250g as possible, of good form and alike in size, shape and colour.

Condition	5 points
Uniformity	3 points
Size	2 points
Shape	3 points
Colour	2 points
TOTAL	15 points

• **Note**: If a class for onions grown from sets is required, the same judging attributes and pointing should be used as for Onions, 250g or under, but with no weight restriction.

Onions, green salad or spring

Merits Fresh, tender leaves, having white unswollen bases with clean roots attached.

Defects Plants that have leaves that are damaged, yellow-tipped or have been trimmed. Plants that have swollen, bulbous bases, coloured other than white.

Advice to judges Look for plants showing good uniformity that are free of pest and disease damage.

Condition	3 points
Uniformity	3 points
Size	2 points
Shape	2 points
Colour	2 points
TOTAL	12 points

Onions on ropes

Onions on ropes are not eligible for collection classes.

Merits Firm, thin-necked blemish-free bulbs grown from either seed or sets with well-ripened, unbroken skins free from pest, disease or other damage. Rope neatly presented, either tied or plaited consisting of 8 bulbs.

Defects Bulbs that are too small, thick-necked, misshapen, blemished, or that have broken skins or have been skinned excessively. Rope untidy or not well presented.

Advice to judges Bulbs should be of good form and alike in size, shape and colour. String or rope of natural material is preferred to tie the onions together.

Condition	5 points
Uniformity	3 points
Size	2 points
Shape	3 points
Colour	2 points
Presentation	5 points
TOTAL	20 points

Judging vegetables

Onions, pickling
Merits Small, firm, well-ripened uniform bulbs, approximately 30mm in diameter.
Defects Bulbs that are soft, unripe, non-uniform, or that are too large or too small, or a poor shape or colour, or have broken skins.
Advice to judges Look for well-formed bulbs of the appropriate size that are firm, uniform and free from any blemish.

Condition	3 points
Uniformity	3 points
Size	2 points
Shape	2 points
Colour	2 points
TOTAL	12 points

Oriental brassicas, flowering stalk types *eg* choi-sum
See **Broccoli, sprouting**, p98.

Oriental brassicas, heading types other than cabbage, Chinese *eg* pak choi types
Merits Fresh, tender, firm, well-developed uniform heads, free from pest or disease damage. Display with roots intact, well washed, wrapped in moist tissues, inserted in a plastic bag and neatly tied.
Defects Poorly formed heads showing evidence of bolting, or pest or disease damage.

Condition	5 points
Uniformity	5 points
Colour	5 points
TOTAL	15 points

Oriental brassicas, loose-leaf or rosette types *eg* leaf mustards, mibuna, mizuna
Merits Fresh, tender, unbroken, well-developed plants, free from pest or disease damage. Display with roots intact, well washed, wrapped in moist tissues, inserted in a plastic bag and neatly tied.
Defects Heads that are limp or show signs of bolting, are blemished or show poor colour.

Condition	5 points
Uniformity	4 points
Colour	3 points
TOTAL	12 points

Parsley
See **Herbs, culinary** p108.

Parsnips

Merits   Long, large well filled and tapered, well developed, shapely white roots, smooth skinned and free from side roots or blemishes and with taproot intact. Foliage trimmed to approximately 75mm.

Defects   Roots that lack size or good, clean shoulders, that are misshapen or have rough, discoloured skins, side roots, blemishes, canker or are excessively ribbed.

Advice to judges   Check that shoulders are symmetrical and free from any blemish. Roots should be fresh, smooth and firm with no blemish or disease, alike in size shape and colour. Good weight is considered more important than length.

Condition	5 points
Uniformity	4 points
Size	4 points
Shape	4 points
Colour	3 points
TOTAL	20 points

Peas

Merits   Large, long, fresh, smooth pods of good colour with bloom intact and with stalks, free from pest or disease damage and well filled with tender peas.

Defects   Pods that are small, not fresh or of poor colour or having very imperfect bloom, or that have no stalks, or that have pest or disease damage or poorly filled or containing peas that are old, pest damaged or have missing peas.

Advice to judges   Look for large, fresh pods, uniform in size, of good colour with bloom intact, pest and disease-free. Open a pod from each exhibit, which should be well filled with blemish-free peas. Where necessary, hold pods up to the light to check for good pod set.

Condition	6 points
Uniformity	4 points
Size	4 points
Shape	4 points
Colour	2 points
TOTAL	20 points

Judging vegetables

Peas, mangetout or snap

Merits Fresh pods of good colour with bloom intact, free from pest or disease damage. Peas should not be overdeveloped.

Defects Pods that are not fresh or of poor colour, or having imperfect bloom, or that are pest or disease damaged, or containing seeds that are poorly set or that are old or maggoty.

Advice to judges For mangetout the pods should be flat with seeds present but undeveloped. For snap peas, pods should be fleshy and snap easily. Where necessary, hold pods up to the light to check for good pod set.

Condition	5 points
Uniformity	4 points
Size	4 points
Colour	2 points
TOTAL	15 points

Pepper, hot (chilli)

Merits Fresh, well developed fruits with uniform colour according to cultivar and stalks attached. Skins should be free of blemishes.

Defects Fruits that are limp or soft to the touch. Fruits showing variation in maturity and colour.

Advice to judges Look for fresh, bright fruits with lustrous colour.

Condition	4 points
Uniformity	3 points
Size	3 points
Shape	2 points
Colour	3 points
TOTAL	15 points

Peppers, sweet

Merits Fresh, brightly coloured fruits, uniform in colour appropriate to the cultivar, free from blemishes, of good size and shape. Clear evidence of a fresh stalk.

Defects Immature, partially coloured fruit. Misshapen fruit displaying poor pollination or having no stalk attached.

Advice to judges Look for uniform, fresh, bright fruits of one good colour with good size and shape.

Condition	5 points
Uniformity	3 points
Size	2 points
Shape	2 points
Colour	3 points
TOTAL	15 points

Potatoes

Merits Medium-sized tubers of approximately 200–250g each; shapely, clean, clear-skinned; eyes few and shallow.

Defects Tubers that are very small or very large, damaged or misshapen, with speckled or patchy skins that are greening or have excessively deep eyes.

Advice to judges Look for clean, blemish-free, medium-sized uniform tubers, well-shaped with shallow eyes.

Condition	5 points
Uniformity	5 points
Size	3 points
Shape	4 points
Eyes	3 points
TOTAL	20 points

Potatoes, salad

See Salad vegetable, miscellaneous, p127.

Pumpkins

Merits A shapely, firm fruit of good colour and ripeness, with stalk attached.

Defects A fruit that is misshapen, soft, unevenly ripened or with a blemished or marked skin, or lacking its stalk.

Advice to judges Look for well-formed, large, shapely fruit that are firm, of good colour and ripeness with stalk attached.

Condition	4 points
Size	3 points
Colour	3 points
TOTAL	10 points

Radishes, Oriental or winter

Merits Fresh roots, well-coloured and free from blemishes.

Defects Roots tough, spongy, of a dull colour or blemished.

Advice to judges Look for roots that are young, tender, uniform and blemish-free.

Condition	5 points
Uniformity	4 points
Size	3 points
Colour	3 points
TOTAL	15 points

Judging vegetables

Radishes, salad

Merits Fresh, firm, young, tender, well-coloured roots, free from blemishes. Foliage trimmed to approximately 30mm.
Defects Roots that are old, tough, misshapen, limp or that show pest or disease damage or evidence of running to seed.
Advice to judges Look for roots that are young, tender, uniform and blemish-free. Size judged according to cultivar.

Condition	4 points
Uniformity	3 points
Size	3 points
Colour	2 points
TOTAL	12 points

Rhubarb, forced

Merits Fresh, firm, straight, long, brightly coloured stalks with well-developed colouring and small, undeveloped leaves.
Defects Stalks that are limp, crooked, small, thin or dull-coloured, or have developed leaf blades or that have had leaves removed.
Advice to judges Look for fresh, firm, straight stalks of uniform overall length and weight with good colour. Foliage should be intact.

Condition	4 points
Uniformity	3 points
Size	3 points
Shape	2 points
Colour	3 points
TOTAL	15 points

Rhubarb, natural

Merits Fresh, straight, long, tender stalks with well-developed colouring with leaf blades trimmed back to approximately 75mm.
Defects Stalks that are small, limp, crooked, stunted, tough, damaged, or lacking in red colouring.
Advice to judges Look for fresh, straight stalks of uniform overall length and weight with good colour. It is advisable to break a stalk in each exhibit to test for freshness and colour.

Condition	3 points
Uniformity	3 points
Shape	3 points
Colour	3 points
TOTAL	12 points

Root vegetables, miscellaneous

See *Root vegetables, miscellaneous*, p127.

Sage

See *Herbs, culinary* p108.

Salad vegetables, miscellaneous
See Salad vegetables, miscellaneous, p127.

Salsify and scorzonera
Merits Large, shapely, evenly tapering, clean, smooth-skinned roots, free from side roots. Scorzonera should be dark in colour. Tops trimmed to approximately 75mm.

Defects Roots that are small, misshapen or taper unevenly or are multi-rooted or lack a clean, smooth skin. Scorzonera roots that are pale.

Advice to judges Look for clean, well-tapered roots that are large without being coarse, and free from blemishes or side roots.

Condition	5 points
Uniformity	4 points
Size	2 points
Shape	2 points
Colour	2 points
TOTAL	15 points

Savory, summer or winter
See Herbs, culinary p108.

Scorzonera
See Salsify and scorzonera, above.

Seakale
Merits Stout, crisp, well-blanched shoots with leaf blades undeveloped.

Defects Shoots that are spindly, limp or poorly blanched or that have developed leaf blades.

Condition	5 points
Uniformity	4 points
Size	2 points
Blanch	2 points
Freedom from leaf-development	2 points
TOTAL	15 points

Shallots, large exhibition

Merits Large, firm, well-ripened, shapely bulbs of good form that are round in cross section, thin necks and of good size and colour.

Defects Bulbs that are not symmetrical or soft or that have thick necks, are poorly ripened or have broken or blemished skins, or bulbs that have been over-skinned.

Advice to judges Pick up each bulb and look for large, shapely, round, uniform, disease-free bulbs that are well presented with tops neatly tied with uncoloured raffia. Over-skinning will reveal greening or purpling of the base. For guidance regarding size see *note*, *p48*.

Condition	6 points
Uniformity	3 points
Size	3 points
Shape	3 points
Colour	3 points
TOTAL	**18 points**

Shallots, pickling

Merits Well-ripened bulbs that are round in cross section and of good form and colour with thin necks. Bulbs must not exceed 30mm in diameter.

Defects Bulbs that are asymmetrical or soft or that have thick necks, are poorly ripened, or have split, broken or blemished skins, or bulbs that have been over-skinned.

Advice to judges Pickling shallots must not exceed 30mm in diameter. Check that each bulb passes through the designated ring easily and unaided. Disqualify exhibits that have oversize bulbs. Ensure that all bulbs are well presented with tops neatly tied with uncoloured raffia. Over-skinning will reveal greening or purpling of the base. For guidance regarding size see *note*, *p48*.

Condition	5 points
Uniformity	4 points
Size	2 points
Shape	2 points
Colour	2 points
TOTAL	**15 points**

Spinach, spinach beet or chard

Merits Fresh, undamaged, well-coloured leaves and stalks. Mixed colours of leaves and stems will be permitted if from a mixed variety.
Defects Leaves that are limp, broken, of poor colour, damaged or diseased.
Advice to judges Look for fresh, large, well-formed leaves of good colour, free from pest or disease damage. Chards should have broad, leaves with good colour appropriate to the cultivar and displayed for effect.

Condition	5 points
Uniformity	3 points
Size	2 points
Colour	2 points
TOTAL	12 points

Spinach, New Zealand

Merits Fresh, dark-green tips without evidence of flowers.
Defects Small, ageing, diseased or yellowing tips or those that show evidence of flowering.
Advice to judges Look for fresh, dark green tips that are approximately 75mm long.

Condition	5 points
Uniformity	2 points
Size	2 points
Colour	3 points
TOTAL	12 points

Squash, summer

See Glossary, p192.
Merits Young, fresh, shapely fruits of any colour but well matched.
Defects Fruits that are not young or fresh or that are misshapen, ill-matched or blemished.
Advice to judges Look for young, tender, shapely fruits. Specimens may be shown with or without flowers attached.

Condition	4 points
Uniformity	3 points
Size	2 points
Shape	3 points
TOTAL	12 points

Squash, winter
See Glossary, p192.
Merits A shapely, large, firm fruit of even colour and ripeness with stalk attached.
Defects A fruit that is misshapen, soft, unevenly ripened or with spotted or marked skin or lacking its stalk.
Advice to judges Look for well-formed, large, shapely fruit that are firm, of good colour and ripeness with stalk attached.

Condition	4 points
Size	3 points
Colour	3 points
TOTAL	10 points

Swedes
Merits Clear-skinned, medium size; well-formed roots free from sideshoots and pests and diseases. Roots should be displayed with approximately 50mm of stalk without leaves.
Defects Roots that are very small or very large have patchy, spongy or cracked skins, of irregular shape or sideshoots.
Advice to Judges Look for medium-sized, well-grown, clean specimens uniform in size shape and colour, pest and disease-free with no evidence of multiple taproots.

Condition	5 points
Uniformity	4 points
Size	2 points
Shape	2 points
Colour	2 points
TOTAL	15 points

Sweet corn
Merits Fresh, cylindrical cobs of good length, well set throughout to the tip, with straight rows of undamaged, plump, tender grains and with fresh green husks.
Defects Cobs that are not fresh or that are unduly tapered or have irregular rows of grain or are badly set or that have husks that are shrivelled and straw-coloured.
Advice to judges Pull down the husks to reveal the grains, which should be fresh, plump and not shrivelled. Well-grown cobs should be well set to the tip.

Condition	5 points
Uniformity	4 points
Size	3 points
Set of grain	3 points
Colour	3 points
TOTAL	18 points

Tarragon
See *Herbs, culinary* p108.

Thyme
See *Herbs, culinary* p108.

Tomatoes, large (*eg* beefsteak type)
Merits Large fruits not less than 75mm in diameter. Shapely, ripe but firm and, well-coloured with fresh calyces attached.
Defects Small, misshapen, unripe or overripe, or of a dull colour, green-backed, evidence of pest or disease damage or lacking calyces.

Condition	5 points
Uniformity	3 points
Size	3 points
Shape	2 points
Colour	2 points
TOTAL	15 points

Tomatoes, medium
Merits Well-shaped, clear-skinned, rounded fruits (approximately 60mm in diameter) ripe but firm. Richly coloured fruits with fresh calyces attached.
Defects Fruits that are small or very large, of uneven shape, unripe or overripe, of a dull colour or green-backed, blemished, or that lack calyces.

Condition	5 points
Uniformity	4 points
Size	3 points
Shape	3 points
Colour	3 points
TOTAL	18 points

Tomatoes, plum
See *Tomatoes, medium*, above (except that they should not be rounded).

Judging vegetables

Tomatoes, small-fruited

Merits Fresh, ripe but firm, well-coloured fruits, blemish-free, and with fresh calyces attached. Size should not exceed 35mm in diameter.

Defects Fruits that are oversize or inappropriately small for the cultivar, or unevenly shaped; unripe or overripe, green-backed or without calyces attached.

Condition	3 points
Uniformity	3 points
Size	2 points
Shape	2 points
Colour	2 points
TOTAL	12 points

Tomatoes, truss

Merits Truss with no fruits missing and free from any pest or disease damage. The truss should gradually reduce or taper down from good quality ripe edible fruits to a number of smaller immature unripe fruits. Single or double trusses are acceptable.

Defects Small truss, misshapen or soft fruit, evidence of pest or disease damage or physiological disorders, uneven ripening, split fruit or fruit ripening out of order along the truss.

Advice to judges The ideal truss would have at least one third of the fruit fully ripe. A truss of tomatoes should not be included in collection classes.

Condition	5 points
Uniformity	3 points
Size	3 points
Shape	2 points
Colour	2 points
TOTAL	15 points

Turnips

Merits Clean, clear skinned solid shapely roots of either ball or flatish type with small single taproots, pest and disease-free, size, shape and colour according to cultivar.

Defects Roots that are very small or very large, have patchy skins, or show evidence of multiple taproots, or are irregular in shape or spongy.

Condition	5 points
Uniformity	4 points
Size	2 points
Shape	2 points
Colour	2 points
TOTAL	15 points

Watercress

See *Salad vegetables, miscellaneous*, p127.

Fruiting vegetables, miscellaneous
eg cucamelons and tomatillos
(*ie* other than those dealt with separately)

Merits Fresh, young, shapely fruits of good uniform shape and colour that are free from pest or disease damage.

Defects Fruits that are not fresh and young, that are misshapen, of poor colour, or that show evidence of pest or disease damage.

Advice to judges Look for ripe, firm, blemish-free, well-coloured fruits of a size according to cultivar with fresh calyces if appropriate.

Condition	4 points
Uniformity	3 points
Size	3 points
Colour	2 points
TOTAL	12 points

Leaf vegetables, miscellaneous
(*ie* other than those dealt with separately)

Merits Fresh, healthy, clean, blemish-free foliage.

Defects Material that is not fresh and clean, is yellowing or showing other signs of age or pest and disease damage.

Advice to judges Look for large, well-formed leaves of good colour, free from pest or disease damage.

Condition	6 points
Size	2 points
Colour	2 points
TOTAL	10 points

Judging vegetables

Root vegetables, miscellaneous (*ie* other than those dealt with separately)
See Glossary, p191.

Merits Clear-skinned, solid, shapely roots that are free of pest and disease damage.

Defects Roots that are very small or very large, have patchy skins, that are spongy, of irregular shape, damaged by pest or disease, or trimmed.

Condition	5 points
Uniformity	4 points
Size	2 points
Shape	2 points
Colour	2 points
TOTAL	15 points

Salad vegetables, miscellaneous (*ie* other than those dealt with separately)
See Glossary, p191.

Merits Material that is young, fresh, clean and of attractive appearance.

Defects Material that is not young or is limp, soiled, pest damaged or at all unattractive.

Advice to judges Look for fresh, clean, young, disease-free specimens that are uniform in size and colour according to type.

Condition	4 points
Uniformity	2 points
Size	2 points
Colour	2 points
TOTAL	10 points

JUDGING FLOWERS AND ORNAMENTAL PLANTS

Specialist shows

The guidance given here applies for local and other non-specialist shows. Specialist plant societies such as the Federation of British Bonsai, British Cactus and Succulent Society, National Chrysanthemum Society, National Dahlia Society, British Fuchsia Society, British Gladiolus Society, British Orchid Council, National Viola and Pansy Society of Great Britain, Royal National Rose Society, National Sweet Pea Society and others may organise their own shows where different rules apply.

Where a scale of points is given in this section it should only apply to that category, and not when different categories are compared.

In assessing the merits of most exhibits of flowers and ornamental plants consideration will be given to the following attributes:

Condition   All material in the exhibit should be at peak condition, clean, fresh and blemish-free

Uniformity   All items in an exhibit should be alike in age, size and form.

Presentation or Staging   The way in which an exhibit of flowers or ornamental plants is staged is important. Although in some cases no points are given for staging, entries should be staged in the most attractive way, which will enhance the show and may influence the judges.

Water   All cut flowers must be staged in water or water-retaining material, such as oasis.

Ornamental bracts   For show purposes, the ornamental bracts around the flowers of plants such as *Euphorbia* (poinsettia), *Bougainvillea*, *Salvia sclarea* (clary) are considered to be part of the flower.

Mixed cultivars are allowed unless otherwise stated.

Judging flowers and ornamental plants

Flowers from annual, biennial, bulbous and herbaceous plants
(other than those for which separate criteria are given elsewhere in this section)

Vases of one kind
Merits   Good fresh condition. A good proportion of flowers fully developed and appropriately positioned on their stem(s). The petals should be properly positioned on the flowers and of a shape, texture and colour typical of the species or cultivar. The foliage should be clean, healthy and undamaged. Stems should be typical of the species or cultivar, and in the case of flowers that bloom in spikes such as larkspurs and hyacinths or in crowns, such as hippeastrums and crown imperials, should be straight and firm right to the tip with the flowers evenly spaced and the open florets touching or almost touching one another.

Defects   Poor condition. Some flowers either undeveloped or past their peak. Petals unnaturally twisted or misshapen or of poor texture or colour for the species or cultivar. Foliage or flowers that are marked or damaged. Stems that are untypically short, twisted, weak or bent.

Advice to judges   For show purposes, the ornamental bracts surrounding the flowers of plants such as *Euphorbia*, *Salvia sclarea* (clary) and *Salvia horminum* are considered to be a part of the flower and the plant may be judged as "in bloom" if these are fully expanded even though the true flowers are not completely open.

Condition of flowers and stems	6 points
Uniformity	4 points
Shape and texture of flowers and foliage	6 points
Colour	4 points
TOTAL	20 points

Mixed vases (ie not less than three different kinds)
The above criteria may be applied equally as well to vases of mixed flowers from different genera, species or cultivars but the judging criteria should be adjusted as follows. The inclusion of foliage from plants other than those of the flowers / berries being exhibited in the mixed vase is not encouraged.

Condition of flowers, foliage and stems	8 points
Colour, texture and arrangement	6 points
Symmetry and balance of exhibit presentation	6 points
TOTAL	20 points

Flowers or fruits from ornamental trees and shrubs (including seedheads)
(other than those for which separate criteria are given elsewhere in this section)

Vases of one kind
Merits Good fresh condition. A good proportion of flowers or fruits fully developed and well positioned on shapely, well-balanced sprays, stems or branches. Individual flowers or fruits well shaped and of a texture, size and colour typical of the species or cultivar. Fresh, healthy, clean, undamaged foliage of good colour and of a size and pattern typical of the species or cultivar.

Defects Poor condition. Flowers or fruits that are misshapen, undeveloped or past their best or sparsely distributed. Sprays, stems or branches that are unevenly developed, unnaturally twisted or stunted or not typical of the species or cultivar. Foliage that is damaged or undersized or oversized for the species or cultivar.

Advice to judges For show purposes, the ornamental bracts surrounding the flowers of plants such as *Cornus kousa*, *Davidia* and *Euphorbia* are considered to be a part of the flower and the plant may be judged as "in bloom" if these are fully expanded even though the true flowers are not completely open.

Condition of flowers/fruit and foliage	5 points
Shape and texture of flowers, fruit and foliage	5 points
Colour	4 points
Stems/sprays/branches	3 points
Balance or symmetry of the exhibit	3 points
TOTAL	20 points

Mixed vases (*ie* not less than three different plants)
The above criteria may be applied equally as well to mixed vases from different genera, species or cultivars, but the judging criteria should be adjusted as shown below. The inclusion of foliage from plants other than those of the flowers/seedheads/fruits being exhibited in the mixed vase is not encouraged.

Condition	8 points
Colour, texture and arrangement	6 points
Symmetry and balance of exhibit presentation	6 points
TOTAL	20 points

Alpine-house and rock-garden plants
Merits A plant of a size suitable for an alpine house or rock garden and hardy enough to survive an average winter in a frost-free house. A plant "in character" (*ie* its character in nature). Many perfect open

blooms in a plant grown for its flower. Closeness and firmness in a cushion plant. Rarity in cultivation. A conifer or a shrub on its own roots should be preferred to a grafted specimen with the exception of certain genera, such as *Pinus*, that are usually propagated by grafting. Colourful foliage in a plant grown for the colour of its leaves.

Defects A plant that is too large to be suitable for an alpine house or rock garden or that is not hardy enough to survive an average winter in an unheated house. A plant that is common in cultivation or easy to grow if in competition with one that is rare in cultivation or difficult to grow. A plant that does not conform to its character in nature. A flowering plant but has few flowers or flowers that are not open or are past their best. A cushion plant that is loose or patchy. A conifer or shrub that has been grafted, with the exception of certain genera, such as *Pinus*, that are usually propagated by grafting, or that has been clipped or artificially dwarfed. A plant grown for its coloured foliage but lacking colour.

Advice to judges A plant need not be a native of mountainous regions and may be a perennial herbaceous plant, an annual or a shrub.

Suitability	2 points
Rarity in cultivation	2 points
In character	2 points
Cultivation	4 points
TOTAL	10 points

Auriculas, alpine, double and show

Merits Well-balanced, healthy foliage. A strong stem, sufficiently long to bear the truss well above the foliage, arising from a single rosette. A truss carried on pedicels sufficiently long to avoid overlapping of the pips. A circular tube, filled by the anthers, hiding the stigma.

• **Alpine auriculas:** a golden, yellow cream or white centre, without farina (a mealy coating). A richly coloured but not necessarily dark edge, shaded to a paler tint.

• **Double auriculas:** the pips should be of rich or clear colours. Doubling to be symmetrical and to fill the corolla effectively. All pips should possess the same degree of doubling.

• **Show auriculas:** a truss consisting of not fewer than five fully developed pips (three in a seedling). A perfectly flat, round, smooth-edged pip consisting of lobes without notches or serrations. Tube of a deep yellow colour. A pure white, smooth paste (inner circular zone of the petals, surrounding the central tube), free from crack or blemish, circular in outline. A dense ground-colour, forming a perfect circle near the paste, the darker and richer the colour the better, though red should not be regarded as a fault. A bright green, grey or white edge of about the same width as the ground-colour. In "selfs" the colour should be uniform throughout and without shading. The paste should be as required in the edged section and should be about equal in width to that of the border colour.

Defects Foliage that is ill-balanced, limp or that has any pest or disease damage. A stem that is weak or short, allowing the pips to overlap. A tube that is irregular or has a visible stigma.

• **Alpine auriculas:** an edge that is not richly coloured.

• **Double auriculas:** pips that are not of rich or clear colours. Doubling that is asymmetrical or lacking effect or shows a marked decrease from the earliest to the latest pip.

• **Show auriculas:** a truss that has fewer than five well-developed pips (three in a seedling). A pip that is not flat, circular or smooth-edged or has fewer than six lobes or has notched or serrated lobes. A tube that is pale-coloured. A paste that is not pure white or is rough, cracked or blemished or lacks a circular outline. A ground-colour that does not have a perfectly circular outline or that lacks density or richness. An edge that is not self-coloured or that is wider than half the width of the paste.

Scales of points

Alpine auriculas

Foliage, stem and pedicels	8 points
Pips	4 points
Tube	2 points
Centre	3 points
Edge	3 points
TOTAL	20 points

Double auriculas

Foliage, stem and pedicels	7 points
Colour of pips	4 points
Doubling: symmetry and effect	6 points
Doubling: degree	3 points
TOTAL	20 points

Show auriculas other than "selfs"

Foliage, stem and pedicels	7 points
Pips	2 points
Tube	2 points
Paste	3 points
Ground-colour	3 points
Edge	3 points
TOTAL	20 points

"selfs"

Foliage, stem and pedicels	7 points
Pips	2 points

Tube	3 points
Paste	4 points
Border	4 points
TOTAL	20 points

Begonias, double tuberous

Merits A well-balanced plant, bearing flowers in size and number proportionate to the size of the plant and to the cultivar. Large flowers of good substance, circular in outline with broad overlapping petals culminating in one centre. Colour decided and clear. In picotee cultivars the colours should not run one into another. Foliage and flowers that are clean, healthy and undamaged. Stems that are stout and erect.

Defects An ill-balanced plant, carrying flowers that are few or small for the size of the plant or the cultivar where known. Small flowers, of poor texture or irregular outline or having divided centres. Long, narrow petals. Pale, damaged or spotted foliage or flowers. Spindly, weak stems.

Advice to judges It is not necessary for the plant to be shown for all-round effect. Supports for the blooms are permitted but should be tidy.

Plant	5 points
Stems	3 points
Form of flower	6 points
Colour	3 points
Foliage	3 points
TOTAL	20 points

Bonsai

A bonsai, meaning a "tree in a tray" in Japanese, is a miniature tree grown in a pot, a miniaturisation of nature and as healthy in all ways as a tree grown in its natural environment. Any tree can be grown as a bonsai but trees with naturally small leaves present a far more pleasing image than those with large leaves; it is possible, with many years of care and training, to reduce the size of leaves but is not possible to reduce the size of fruits and flowers.

Merits A strong, well-shaped trunk tapering upwards and merging naturally with the growing medium. Surface roots may fan out from the base of the trunk and gradually disappear into the soil. Well-proportioned head of branches well-spaced and set on the trunk with a natural apex and without obvious scars or marks of training. A tree looking as natural as possible with all its parts in proportion. A tree with well-presented growing medium and showing stability in the pot, which should be of an appropriate colour and type and in proportion to the height and girth of the tree. The tree should be

a healthy colour showing evidence of vitality and growth while retaining its shape and showing evidence of care and attention with no evidence of damage.
Defects Weak, badly shaped or inverted taper in trunks and those that look like sticks stuck in the ground. Badly spaced, cut, scarred or crossed branches. Evidence of damage. Noticeable artificial training; uncharacteristic growth for species. Snagged or abruptly cut roots visible above the soil or dead fibrous roots standing in the air. Trees out of balance. Flowers, fruit or foliage out of proportion to the size of the tree. Soil surface and bole of trunk sunk well below the rim of the pot. Unnecessary additional ornaments or decoration.
Advice to judges Wiring on the trunk and branches is permissible but it should be neat and not obvious and with no signs of the wire cutting into the branch tissue. Pots for coniferous trees are generally brown, or occasionally grey, unglazed pots and for deciduous trees are glazed and of a muted colour.

Cacti and succulents

The suggestions below are for use at smaller shows. For specialist shows, British Cactus and Succulent Society (www.bcss.org.uk) rules may apply.
Merits A large specimen for the particular species, hybrid or cultivar; well-balanced and in good health. It should be free from defects of any sort including damaged or missing spines, distorted bodies or leaves, abnormal marks or lesions (except close to soil level), or defective "bloom". A species, hybrid or cultivar that is difficult to cultivate will be preferred to one that is easy. Pot size appropriate to the size of plant.
Defects A specimen that is small for the particular species, hybrid or cultivar, is in poor health or shows evidence of pest infestation at any time in its life. A specimen that has damaged or missing spines, distortion of bodies or leaves, scarring of body or leaves, defective "bloom" or that is poorly presented. A specimen of flowering size that shows no evidence of flowering, if in competition with one that does. Plant over- or under-potted.
Advice to Judges While the condition, maturity and rarity of the plant are important, for local shows, plants in flower or showing evidence that they have flowered are to be preferred. Cacti are classified as succulents (see **Glossary**, p193)

Condition	6 points
Maturity (age in cultivation)	5 points
Freedom from pests and diseases	2 points
Difficulty of cultivation	3 points
Rarity in cultivation	1 points
Presentation	3 points
TOTAL	20 points

Carnations, border (including picotees)

Border carnations may be classed according to colour as follows:
"Selfs": must be of one clear colour.
Fancies: must have a clear ground-colour and be marked or suffused by a contrasting colour or colours.
Picotees: must have a clear ground-colour, with an even, unbroken margin of contrasting colour around every petal.
Fancies and *picotees* may be further divided according to their ground-colour. Cloves may be any colour or colours, but must possess a strong clove scent.

Merits Good condition. Flowers that are fresh, symmetrical and circular in outline, with no hole or gap in the centre. Firm petals with smooth edges, slight indentation permitted. Guard-petals that are large, broad, smooth and carried at right angles to the calyx. Inner petals that lie regularly and smoothly over the guard-petals, though the centre petals may stand up somewhat and form a crown. Calyx should be unbroken. Strong stems. Colour or colours clear, bright and well defined. A strong scent. Uniformity.

Defects Unsatisfactory condition. Holes or gaps should not appear in the centre of the flower. Flowers that are small or not circular in outline. Petals that lack substance or have serrated edges or show a marked tendency to incurve or are so numerous as to appear crowded. Guard-petals that are small, narrow or are incurved or recurved. Split calyces and stems that are weak or lacking uniformity.

Advice to Judges Unless permitted by the schedule, exhibits with stem supports or calyx bands must be disqualified.

Condition	6 points
Form (of flower)	6 points
Size	3 points
Colour	3 points
Presentation and staging	2 points
TOTAL	20 points

Carnations, perpetual-flowering

Perpetual-flowering carnations may be classed according to colour as follows:
"Selfs": which must be of one clear colour.
Fancies: must have a clear ground-colour and be marked or suffused with a contrasting colour or colours.
Fancies may be further divided according to their ground-colour.

Merits Good condition. Flowers that are large, symmetrical circular in outline and that have full centres. Guard-petals that are flat, firm and well formed. (The edges may be either smooth or regularly serrated.) Calyx unbroken. Strong stems proportionate in length and thickness to the size of the flowers. Clear and bright colours. A strong scent. Uniformity.

Defects Unsatisfactory condition. Flowers that are coarse, small or asymmetrical. Split calyces with weak, clumsy or short stems, lacking scent and uniformity.

Advice to Judges Unless permitted by the schedule, exhibits with stem supports or calyx bands must be disqualified.

Condition	6 points
Form (of flower)	6 points
Size	3 points
Colour	3 points
Presentation and staging	2 points
TOTAL	20 points

Chrysanthemums

For shows organised by the National Chrysanthemum Society (NCS) or for chrysanthemum classes in shows organised by societies affiliated to the NCS, the use of the NCS scale of points may be obligatory. Details of these scales may be obtained from the Secretary of the National Chrysanthemum Society (www.nationalchrysanthemumsociety.co.uk).

The following paragraphs contain advice about judging most of the different sections into which chrysanthemum cultivars have been classified.

Classification
Late-flowering (indoor cultivars)

Section 1	Large exhibition (incurving and reflexing)
Section 2	Medium exhibition
Section 3	Exhibition incurved
Section 4	Reflexed decoratives
Section 5	Intermediate decoratives
Section 6	Anemones
Section 7	Singles
Section 8	Pompons
Section 9	Sprays
Section 10	Spiders, Quills, Spoons
Section 11	Any other types

Judging flowers and ornamental plants

October-flowering
Section 13	Incurved decoratives
Section 14	Reflexed decoratives
Section 15	Intermediate decoratives
Section 16	Large anemones, October-flowering
Section 17	Singles, October-flowering
Section 18	Pompons, October-flowering
Section 19	Sprays, October-flowering
Section 20	Any other types, October-flowering

Early-flowering (outdoor cultivars)
Section 21	Koreans and Rubellums
Section 22	Garden charms
Section 23	Incurved decoratives
Section 24	Reflexed decoratives
Section 25	Intermediate decoratives
Section 26	Anemones
Section 27	Singles
Section 28	Pompons
Section 29	Sprays
Section 30	Any other types

Cultivars in Sections 13 to 20 (October-flowering types) may normally be shown in classes at shows for early-flowering types but those in Sections 13 to 16 may also usually be shown in classes at shows for late-flowering types. Early-flowering chrysanthemums (Sections 23 to 30) include all cultivars that in a normal season bloom in the open ground before 1 October. Though these blooms must be grown in the open it is usually permissible to protect them from weather damage.

It is permissible for canes, neatly tied, to be used to support the stems of chrysanthemums of all sections. The supports should be unobtrusive so as not to detract from the exhibit.

Sections 1 and 2: Late-flowering large and medium exhibition
• **Note:** rings may be used to support the blooms.
Merits Reflexing types: a bloom in which the breadth and depth are approximately equal and that has good shoulders and a full centre. Florets (which may be either flat and broad or quilled) gracefully reflexed, of good substance, fresh to the tips, unspoiled and of bright colour. Incurving types: a bloom that is globular or nearly so, with a full centre. Florets that are broad incurved (either closely and regularly or loosely and irregularly), fresh to the tips and of bright colour.
Defects A bloom that is much broader than deep or lacks good shoulders, is coarse or has a depressed centre. Florets that are not gracefully reflexed, are of poor substance, stale (no longer fresh) at the tips, spotted or of dull colour or drooping.
Points *See pp141*

Sections 3, 13 and 23: Incurved decoratives
Merits A bloom that is compact and globular or nearly so. Florets that are broad, smooth, rounded at the tips, of sufficient length to form a graceful curve, closely and regularly arranged, firm, fresh (including the outer ones) and of a clear, decisive colour.

Defects A bloom that is loose, flat, has a hollow centre or is irregular in outline. Florets that are narrow, loosely or irregularly arranged, soft, lacking freshness or of dull or undecided colour.

• **Note:** No cups or rings are permissible but, in Section 3, the stem may be supported.

Points *See pp141*

Sections 4, 14 and 24: Reflexed decoratives
Merits Blooms that are broad and deep and have full centres. Florets of good substance, bright in colour and fresh to the tips. Florets that reflex gracefully and overlap one another perfectly.

In types with quilled, sharply pointed florets that stand out stiffly, freshness to the tips is of particular importance.

Defects Blooms that are narrow or shallow or lack full centres or have daisy-eyes, ie visible disc-florets. Florets that are of poor substance, stale, drooping, dull in colour, ragged or misplaced.

Points *See pp141*

Section 5, 15 and 25: Intermediate decoratives
Merits Blooms that are globular in outline, with breadth and depth approximately equal. Florets that are broad, incurving (either closely and regularly or loosely and irregularly), of good substance, fresh to the tips and of bright colour. In semi-reflexing types, a pleasing contrast in colour between the outer reflexing and the inner recurving florets.

Defects Blooms that are too broad for their depth and not globular in outline. Florets that are narrow, of poor substance, stale or of dull colour.

Points *See pp141*

Sections 6, 16 and 26:
Merits Blooms that have fresh, deep, symmetrical "cushions" (ie discs) of even size and bright colour. Ray-florets that are fresh and of bright colour: either broad to the tips, flat and of equal length or pointed and of uneven size.

Defects Blooms with cushions that are stale, shallow, malformed, of uneven size or dull colour. Ray-florets that are drooping or not fresh to the tips or of a dull colour.

Points *See pp141*

Sections 7, 17 and 27: Singles
Blooms with approximately five rows of ray-florets.

Merits Flowers borne at right angles to the stems. Ray-florets that are broad, flat, of good substance, fresh to the tips and of a bright colour. Disc-florets that are fresh, clear and regular.
Defects Flowers that are not borne at right angles to the stems. Ray-florets in excess or that are narrow, incurving or not flat or are of poor substance, drooping or stale. Disc-florets that are old, dull or irregular. Slight reflexing or incurving at the tips of ray-florets should be regarded as defective in some cultivars.
Points *See pp141*

Sections 8, 18 and 28: Pompons
Merits Blooms that are symmetrical (ball-shaped), with full centres, of uniform size and bright colour.
Defects Blooms that are asymmetrical, lack full centres, are of uneven size or of a dull colour.
Points *See pp141 & 142*

Sections 9, 19 and 29: Sprays
A spray for the purposes of these sections is the last flowering growth consisting of one stem (not a branch) with or without a central flower bud.
Merits The blooms of sprays should be fresh, clean, of uniform size, development and colour. Individual blooms evenly spaced and not overlapping one another. Foliage small, fresh and clean.
Defects Dead or faded blooms, colour variation and poor foliage.
Points *See pp141 & 142*

Scales of points

Sections 3, 4, 5, 6, 7, 11, 13, 14, 15, 16, 17, 20, 23, 24, 25, 26, 27 and 30, and sections 8, 9, 18, 19, 28 and 29 when shown as individual blooms

Form	6 points
Size	4 points
Freshness	4 points
Colour	2 points
Uniformity between blooms of cultivar	2 points
Foliage	1 point
Staging	1 point
TOTAL	20 points

Sections 1 and 2

Form	5 points
Size	6 points
Freshness	6 points
Colour	2 points
Staging and foliage	1 point
TOTAL	20 points

Section 10

Form	6 points
Size	5 points
Freshness	5 points
Colour	2 points
Staging	1 point
Foliage	1 point
TOTAL	20 points

Natural sprays from sections 8, 9, 18, 19, 28 and 29

Bloom quality:

Form	3 points
Freshness	5 points
Colour	3 points
Overall effect (including progression of development and staging)	8 points
Foliage	1 point
TOTAL	20 points

Exhibition sprays from sections 8, 9, 18, 19, 28 and 29

Bloom quality:

Form	3 points
Freshness	4 points
Colour	2 points
Size	1 point
Spray quality:	
Form	3 points
Uniform placement and development	3 points
Overall effect (including staging and number of blooms)	3 points
Foliage	1 point
TOTAL	20 points

Chrysanthemums, specimen plants in pots

Merits A symmetrical plant, "facing all round", with a single main stem for not less than 25mm between the soil and the first branch or break. Blooms numerous and of high quality. Foliage ample, clean and healthy. Stems that have been bent gradually from near their bases. Supports and ties inconspicuous. There should be not less than 45mm of clear stem between soil level and the bottom of the head in standard pompons and not less than 60mm in standards of large-flowered cultivars.

Defects A plant that is not symmetrical or faces only one way or has more than one main stem immediately above the soil. Blooms that are not sufficiently numerous for the size of the plant or are lacking in quality. Stems that have been bent abruptly. Supports or ties that are obtrusive or ties too near the blooms.

Number, quality and freshness of blooms	10 points
Foliage	4 points
Training	6 points
TOTAL	20 points

Chrysanthemums, cascade
Merits   A well-trained and balanced plant, evenly furnished with fully open blooms that are fresh and bright in colour. Training frames, canes and ties should be as inconspicuous as possible.
Defects   A badly trained, unevenly balanced plant with few blooms open or with blooms past their best and fading. Training frames, canes and ties that are conspicuous or badly positioned.

Number, quality and freshness of blooms	8 points
Foliage	2 points
Training	10 points
TOTAL	20 points

Chrysanthemums, charm and cushion
Merits   A symmetrical plant "facing all round", evenly furnished with fully open blooms that are fresh and bright in colour. Foliage clean and healthy. Plant size commensurate with the size of the pot.
Defects   A plant that is not symmetrical or faces only one way, or is unevenly furnished with a low proportion of open blooms, or having flowers that are faded and dull. A loose open plant.

Number, quality and freshness of blooms	10 points
Foliage	4 points
Training	6 points
TOTAL	20 points

Daffodils (*Narcissus*)
Merits   Flower carried at nearly a right angle to the stem, except in species and hybrids where a pendent flower is typical, such as *Narcissus triandrus* and its hybrids. Perianth of smooth texture and good substance. Segments broad and overlapping from the base for a good proportion of their length, flat or slightly twisted symmetrically in each segment or in alternate segments. Corona or crown of good colour, texture and substance, proportionate to the perianth in length and width, any frill or flange at the brim being even and uniform. Stem straight and strong and proportionate in length to the size of the flower. Perianth and corona symmetrical. Neck of flower short. In double cultivars, segments and colour symmetrically arranged.
Defects   (Note: These defects would not necessarily all apply to species.) A flower that is immature or over-mature, or in which the colours are faded or burnt, or in which the perianth or corona is not symmetrical. A flower or stem that shows signs of damage or disease.

A flower that faces downwards, except in species and hybrids in which a pendent flower is typical. A perianth of poor or uneven colour, ribbed, thin or hooded. Segments that are too narrow to overlap for a good proportion of their length or that are neither flat nor symmetrically twisted, or that have notches, nicks or tears. A corona or crown of poor colour, texture or substance or that has a frill or flange that is uneven or has spots at the margin. A stem that is weak or bent and disproportionate in length to the flower. A long neck. In double cultivars, segments or colour unevenly distributed. A vase containing more than one stem in which the flowers are not uniform. No artificial support or wiring of blooms is allowed.

Scale of points

The following scale should be used as a guide to the relative importance of the features of an exhibit. In classes for more than one vase, each vase should be judged and marked individually. Before this is done, the exhibit as a whole should be marked out of an additional 10 percent of total points for visual impact and coverage of divisions and colour combinations. For example, in a class of six vases of single blooms judges should mark out of 10 for each vase, total 60 points, having first marked out of an additional 6 points (10 percent) for impact of the group and diversity.

In a class for single blooms

Form and poise	3 points
Colour	2 points
Condition and texture	2 points
Stem	1 point
Size (for the cultivar)	1 points
Presentation	1 point
TOTAL	10 points

In a class with three or more blooms to a vase add 2 points for uniformity to the above.

In a class for daffodils exhibited in growth in pots, pans or bowls

Form, colour, size (for the cultivar), texture and poise of the blooms	4 points
Condition and cleanliness of the blooms and foliage	3 points
Impact, symmetry and uniformity	3 points
TOTAL	10 points

Classification of *Narcissus*

The following classification of daffodils has been adopted by the Royal Horticultural Society:

Judging flowers and ornamental plants

Division 1 Trumpet daffodils
One flower to a stem; corona (trumpet) as long as or longer than the perianth segments (petals).

Division 2 Large-cupped daffodils
One flower to a stem; corona (cup) more than one-third, but less than equal to the length of the perianth segments (petals).

Division 3 Small-cupped daffodils
One flower to a stem; corona (cup) not more than one-third the length of the perianth segments (petals).

Division 4 Double daffodils
One or more flowers to a stem, with doubling of the perianth segments or the corona or both.

Division 5 Triandrus daffodils
Characteristics of *Narcissus triandrus* clearly evident: usually two or more pendent flowers to a stem; perianth segments reflexed.

Division 6 Cyclamineus daffodils
Characteristics of *Narcissus cyclamineus* clearly evident: one flower to a stem; perianth segments significantly reflexed; flower at an acute angle to the stem, with a very short pedicel (neck).

Division 7 Jonquilla and Apodanthus daffodils
Characteristics of sections Jonquilla or Apodanthi clearly evident: one to five (rarely eight) flowers to a stem; perianth segments spreading or reflexed; corona cup-shaped, funnel-shaped or flared, usually wider than long; flowers usually fragrant.

Division 8 Tazetta daffodils
Characteristics of section Tazettae clearly evident: usually three to 20 flowers to a stout stem; perianth segments spreading, not reflexed; flowers usually fragrant.

Division 9 Poeticus daffodils
Characteristics of *Narcissus poeticus* and related species clearly evident; perianth segments pure white; corona very short or disc-shaped, not more than one-fifth the length of the perianth segments; corona usually with a green and/or yellow centre and red rim, but sometimes wholly or partly of other colours; anthers usually set at two distinct levels; flowers fragrant.

Division 10 Bulbocodium daffodils
Characteristics of section Bulbocodium clearly evident; usually one flower to a stem; perianth segments insignificant compared with the dominant corona; anthers dorsifixed (attached more-or-less centrally to the filament); filament and style usually curved.

Division 11 Split-corona daffodils
Corona split, usually for more than half its length.

11a Collar daffodils have the corona segments opposite the perianth segments; the corona segments usually in two whorls of three.

11b Papillon daffodils have the corona segments alternate to the perianth segments; the corona segments usually in a single whorl of six.

Judging flowers and ornamental plants

Division 12 Other daffodils of garden origin
Daffodils which do not fit the definition of any other division.

Division 13 Daffodils distinguished solely by botanical name
Note: the characteristics for Divisions 5 to 10 are given for guidance only; they are not all necessarily expected to be present in every cultivar.

Intermediate and miniature
   Intermediate daffodils: between 51 and 80mm in diameter
   Miniature daffodils: up to 50mm in diameter

Perianth and corona colour
Where a class requires blooms to have a yellow-orange or white perianth or corona, the perianth or corona must be predominantly, but not necessarily exclusively, that colour

Rim
Rimmed daffodils are those which display at the corona rim a clearly defined band of colour that is different from the colour or colours of the corona base and mid-zone.

Dahlias

The following paragraphs were prepared in consultation with the National Dahlia Society (NDS; www.dahlia-nds.co.uk).
Merits Bloom fresh and clean, all florets intact, firm and without blemish or defect. Colour(s) clear and well-defined, and either consistent or evenly shaded or tipped throughout the bloom. The following standards may also be used when judging the different categories:

Single and Collerette dahlias
Eight or more outer florets, possibly overlapping but not assuming double formation, equal in size, uniform in shape and formation, radiating evenly and regularly away from the central disc in a single flat plane with the outer edges rounded or pointed. Inner florets or collar of Collerettes not less than one third of the length of the outer florets, even in colour and formation. Central disc flat and circular, containing not more than two rows of pollen-bearing stamens. Bloom poised at an angle of not less than 45 degrees to the stem, which should be straight and proportionate to the size of the bloom.

Anemone-flowered dahlias
Close and compact group of tubular florets comprising the centre of the bloom, circular in outline. Outer ray-florets equal in size, uniform in shape and formation, generally flat and regularly arranged around

the central florets. Bloom poised at an angle of not less than 45 degrees to the stem, which should be straight and proportionate to the size of the bloom.

Waterlily dahlias
Blooms should be fully double and the face view circular in outline and regular in arrangement. A firm, circular, closed centre, proportionate to the size of the flower. The depth of the bloom should be approximately half the diameter. Bloom poised at an angle of not less than 45 degrees to the stem, which should be straight and of a length and thickness proportionate to the size of the bloom.

Decorative, Cactus and Semi-cactus dahlias
Bloom symmetrical and outline perfectly circular. A firm, circular, closed centre, proportionate to the size of the flower. Bloom "full", having, without overcrowding, sufficient florets to prevent gaps in formation and outline and to give depth to the bloom, which should be approximately two thirds, or more, of the diameter. Bloom poised at an angle of not less than 45 degrees to the stem, which should be straight and of a length and thickness proportionate to the size of the bloom. The formation of blooms and their florets should correspond to the standards laid down for that particular class of dahlia.

Ball dahlias
Blooms should be ball-shaped but the tendency towards flatness on the face of the larger cultivars is acceptable. Ray-florets compact and dense at the centre, symmetrically arranged, dressing back to the stem to complete the ball shape of the bloom. Florets compact and dense at the centre. Bloom poised at an angle of not less than 45 degrees to the stem, which should be straight and of a length and thickness proportionate to the size of the bloom.

Pompon dahlias
Bloom perfectly globular. Florets involute for the whole of their length, evenly and symmetrically arranged throughout the bloom and dressing back fully to the stem. Bloom facing upwards on a straight, firm stem.

Miscellaneous dahlias
Blooms equal in size and uniform in formation. Bloom poised at an angle of not less than 45 degrees to the stem, which should be straight and proportionate to the size of the bloom.

Fimbriated dahlias
Fully double blooms. Petals split or notched uniformly throughout the bloom, to create a fringed overall effect. Petals may be flat, involute, revolute, straight, incurving or twisted. Bloom poised at an

angle of not less than 45 degrees to the stem, which should be straight and proportionate to the size of the bloom.

Star and Double orchid dahlias
Blooms equal in size and uniform in formation. Bloom poised at an angle of not less than 45 degrees to the stem, which should be straight and proportionate to the size of the bloom.

Paeony dahlias
Blooms equal in size and uniform in formation. Outer ray florets equal in shape, size and formation, generally flat and regularly arranged around the central disc. Bloom poised at an angle of not less than 45 degrees to the stem, which should be straight and proportionate to the size of the bloom.

Exhibits
An exhibit of dahlias should be so arranged that all the blooms face in the same direction, are clear of each other and a pleasant and balanced effect is achieved. Blooms should be staged with some dahlia foliage, preferably on the stem. The foliage should be clean, healthy and undamaged. The names of all cultivars in an exhibit should be clearly stated.

Defects As a general principle anything that detracts from the perfection of a bloom, or an exhibit, is a fault and the seriousness or otherwise of the fault depends on the degree of imperfection. In judging an exhibit the following faults should be evaluated.

It is a very serious fault if a bloom is malformed, faces downwards, has been badly damaged, has limp drooping florets, has had an excessive number of florets removed, has an open (daisy-eyed) centre (double flowered cultivars only), has a centre that is hard and green, large and undeveloped or badly distorted, has a gap created by a missing outer floret (Groups 1–3 only), or seriously departs from the standard formation of the class of dahlia for which the class calls.

The following faults may be either minor or serious, in accordance with the amount by which the fault detracts from the perfection of a bloom: oval, sunken or isolated centres, irregular or oval outline of bloom, uneven, irregular, or unbalanced formation, florets lacking freshness or bleached, discoloured, faded, eaten, bruised, malformed or otherwise blemished, where florets have been removed, stems that are bent, weak, short-jointed, thick or out of proportion, uneven or inconsistent colouring (except bicoloured blooms), shallow blooms, *ie* those lacking depth of fullness (except Groups 1, 3 and 4), blooms that are immature or past their best, or the presence of pests.

Angle of bloom (Group 7): the bloom of a pompon dahlia should face upwards on a straight, firm stem. Any variation should be regarded as a fault. When several blooms are shown together in an exhibit, it is a fault for them to face at different angles.

Disqualification must result for any of the following reasons:
1. Blooms of large-flowered dahlias exceeding 260mm;
   Blooms of medium-flowered dahlias exceeding 220mm;
   Blooms of small-flowered dahlias exceeding 170mm;
   Blooms of miniature-flowered dahlias exceeding 115mm;
   Blooms of large pompon dahlias exceeding 83mm;
   Blooms of pompon dahlias exceeding 55mm.
2. Blooms artificially supported above the top level of the vase.
3. Incorrect number of blooms in an exhibit, including buds whether embryo or showing colour. All buds are treated as blooms and will result in disqualification if not removed over the correct number.
4. Classified blooms exhibited in wrong class.
5. If a vase in a multi-vase exhibit is not according to schedule (NAS) then the whole exhibit must be disqualified. While the whole exhibit cannot be considered for an award, awards to individual vases, other than the disqualified vases, are permitted (*eg* best vase in its group in that exhibit).

Pointing The NDS does not favour the use of a scale of points for judging. The RHS considers that in certain cases such a scale may provide a useful guide and the following scale is accordingly suggested for use if desired.

Form and centre	5 points
Condition	10 points
Stem	3 points
Colour	2 points
TOTAL	20 points

Classification of *Dahlia*
The NDS produces a classified list of cultivars. A cultivar can only be shown in a class in which it is classified. NDS classifications are as follows:

Group 1 Single flowered dahlias
Single dahlias have blooms with a single outer ring of florets, which may overlap, the centre forming a disc.

Group 2 Anemone-flowered dahlias
Anemone-flowered dahlias have blooms with one or more outer rings of generally flattened ray florets surrounding a dense group of tubular florets, and showing no disc.

Judging flowers and ornamental plants

Group 3 Collerette dahlias
Collerette dahlias have blooms with a single outer ring of generally flat ray florets, which must overlap, with a ring of small florets (the collar) in the centre forming a disc.

Group 4 Waterlily dahlias
Waterlily dahlias have fully double blooms characterised by broad ray florets that are slightly involute along their length (longitudinal axis) giving a saucer shaped appearance to the bloom. The depth should be not more than one third of the diameter of the bloom.

Group 5 Decorative dahlias
Decorative dahlias have fully double blooms showing no disc. The ray florets are generally broad and flat and may be involute for no more than 75 percent of their length (longitudinal axis) or slightly twisted, and usually bluntly pointed.

Group 6 Ball dahlias
Ball dahlias have fully double blooms, ball shaped or slightly flattened. The ray florets rounded at the tips, with margins spirally arranged and involute for at least 75 percent of the length of the florets.

Group 7 Pompon dahlias
Pompon dahlias have fully double spherical blooms of miniature size, with florets largely involute along their length (longitudinal axis).

Group 8 Cactus dahlias
Cactus dahlias have fully double blooms, the ray florets are usually pointed, the majority narrow and revolute for 65 percent or more of their length (longitudinal axis) and either straight or incurving.

Group 9 Semi-cactus dahlias
Semi-Cactus dahlias have fully double blooms; the ray florets are usually pointed and revolute for more than 25 percent and less than 65 percent of their length and broad at the base and either straight or incurving.

Group 10 Miscellaneous dahlias
Any dahlias which do not fall into Groups 1–9 inclusive or Groups 11, 12,13 & 14, such as Thistle Dahlias, etc. This group includes *Dahlia* species.

Group 11 Fimbriated dahlias
Fimbriated dahlias have blooms where the tips of the ray florets should be evenly split or notched into two or more divisions, uniformly throughout the bloom to create a fringed overall effect. The petals may be flat, involute, revolute, straight, incurving or twisted.

Group 12 Star dahlias
Star dahlias have blooms with a single outer ring of florets surrounding the disc. Ray florets are uniformly either involute or revolute.

Group 13 Double orchid dahlias
Double orchid dahlias have fully double blooms showing no disc and have triangular centres. Ray florets are narrowly lance shaped and either involute or revolute.

Group 14 Paeony dahlias
Paeony dahlias have multiple outer rings of ray florets surrounding a disc, ray florets are flat or slightly involute at base and are flat or are to some extent revolute.

The 2015 *National Dahlia Society Classified Directory* has subdivided **Groups 4, 5, 8, 9 and 11** for show purposes as follows:

Giant:	more than 250mm in diameter
Large:	between 200 and 250mm in diameter
Medium:	between 150 and 200mm in diameter
Small:	between 100 and 150mm in diameter
Miniature:	not exceeding 100mm in diameter

Group 6 is subdivided for show purposes as follows:

Small Ball:	between 100 and 150mm in diameter
Miniature Ball:	between 50 and 100mm in diameter

Group 7 is subdivided for show purposes as follows:

Large Pompon:	between 50 and 75mm in diameter
Pompon:	must not exceed 55mm in diameter

Judging flowers and ornamental plants

Delphiniums, spikes
Merits Spikes that are in good condition. Long, tapering or columnar in shape, with at least two thirds of florets open, and staged with a minimum of 100mm of stem visible below the bottom florets. Florets of good substance and colour, whether of self, contrasting colour or striped, showing good placement. Well-furnished florets of circular outline with neat and even "eye" petals are preferred. Presentation is important, with staging carried out to present an upright spike with clean foliage inserted to conceal packing.
Defects Unsatisfactory condition. Spikes that are underdeveloped, crooked or malformed, or that are sparsely or irregularly furnished with florets, or are overcrowded. Florets that are small, or that have faded or fallen petals. Signs of stripped florets or conspicuous seed pods. Unsatisfactory presentation.
Advice to judges Delphinium spikes are preferably shown with sideshoots removed.

Condition	5 points
Form and size of spike	5 points
Florets	5 points
Overall effect	5 points
TOTAL	20 points

Additional points in multi-vase classes:

Uniformity	3 points
TOTAL	23 points

Delphiniums, displayed florets
These should be presented as directed in the show schedule.
Merits *See Delphiniums, spikes*. Uniformity is of added importance when florets only are displayed.
Defects *See Delphiniums, spikes*

Condition	5 points
Substance and clarity of colour	5 points
Size and uniformity	5 points
Presentation	5 points
TOTAL	20 points

Floating flowers
This section applies to classes for floating flowers, usually shown in a bowl.
Merits Undamaged flowers of a size typical of the cultivar. Symmetrical arrangement filling the container.
Defects Flowers damaged or materially overlapping each other. Unbalanced arrangement. Flowers that are not floating.
Advice to Judges The decorative effect is as important as the condition of the flowers. Gently move the container to ensure that

the flowers are floating.

Condition	8 points
Decorative effect	8 points
Uniformity	4 points
TOTAL	20 points

Floral arrangements

Fashions in the design of such floral arrangements as baskets, vases, bowls, bouquets and dinner-table decorations change considerably from one period to another, as does the range of flowers and foliage used. Beauty of form and colour, lightness of arrangement, happy harmonies or suitable contrasts always meet with general approval. The use of suitable foliage, berries, fruits and seed pods and accessories may be desirable and permitted or required by the schedule. The rarity and cost of the flowers should not, as such, influence judges.

The schedule will usually convey whether the class is interpretative or a straightforward arrangement, and may indicate whether the judges should be guided by rules and definitions formulated by National Association of Flower Arrangement Societies (www.nafas.org.uk).

Fuchsia blooms

The following paragraphs were prepared in consultation with the British Fuchsia Society (www.thebfs.org.uk).

Merits Flowers that are fully open and complete with all floral parts. All floral parts except the anthers should be free of pollen. The stigma should be fresh. The anthers should be at the stage of development where pollen is about to appear or has just appeared.

Defects Flowers that are dirty or damaged. Flowers that are premature, not fully open, incomplete or immature. Flowers that have more or less than four sepals except where normal for that cultivar. Anthers that have lost their pollen. A stigma that has wilted or died.

Advice to judges Check that each flower has four sepals except where normal for that cultivar, that each bloom is fresh and typical of the cultivar. Look for a well-balanced, clean exhibit with pollen on the anthers and with fresh stigmas.

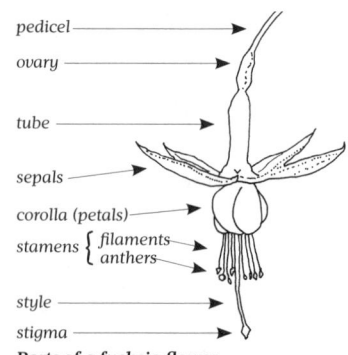

Parts of a fuchsia flower
Diagram courtesy British Fuchsia Society

Condition	4 points
Size (according to cultivar)	2 points
Colour	2 points
Presentation	2 points
TOTAL	10 points

Fuchsias

Fuchsias can be shown in several forms as follows:

Bush: a plant which must be seen to have been developed in a single stem not exceeding 40mm.

Shrub: a plant with more than one shoot emerging from below compost level.

Standards: all standards must have a stem clear of all growth from compost level to the first branch. The stem may be supported by a single stake. The stem lengths, measured from compost level to the underside of the first branch should be as follows:

Full standard:	between 760mm and 1070mm
Half standard:	between 460mm and 760mm
Quarter standard:	between 250mm and 460mm
Mini standard:	between 150mm and 250mm.

Other trained shapes: other shapes such as espalier, fan, pillar, conical, pyramid, ring, etc may be developed.

Merits A vigorous, symmetrical or balanced, floriferous plant, well furnished with clean and fresh blooms and foliage of good colour. Leaves free of nectar and pollen. For standards, the whole of the exhibit should be in proportion – the size of the pot, length of stem and diameter and depth of the head, ie diameter of the head should be approximately three times the diameter of the pot. Support and ties (if any) neat and unobtrusive. The length of clear stem within the recommended ranges for its group. Stems should be straight, free of blemishes (tie marks, etc). For trained shapes the framework should be covered by plant growth and remain inconspicuous and the shape readily recognisable.

Defects A plant that is stunted, ill-balanced or sparsely flowered or that has poor or dirty foliage or has blooms that are not sufficiently open or past their best or that has untidy or obtrusive supports or ties or that has incorrect stem lengths for its group. A trained shape where the framework is overly visible and the shape not easily recognisable. A plant that shows evidence of pest or disease damage.

Quality and quantity of bloom	8 points
Quality and quantity of foliage	5 points
Cultural quality	5 points
Presentation	2 points
TOTAL	20 points

Gladiolus, non-primulinus

The following paragraphs were prepared in consultation with the British Gladiolus Society (www.britglad.com).

Merits An erect spike, with fresh, unblemished blooms and foliage. A long, well-balanced spike according to cultivar, still carrying the bottom flower with numerous regularly spaced open and opening flowers and buds, so placed as to hide the stem and gradually narrowing from base to top. An ideal spike would be approximately one third in full flower, one third with buds in colour and one third in green bud. Flowers that are typical of the cultivar and of good form, texture and colour, free from damage and uneven and irregular markings.

Defects A spike that is bent or has a drooping tip, or carries old or blemished flowers or empty bracts or a spike from which a bract has been removed or one with blemished foliage. A short, ill-balanced or crowded spike giving the appearance of having too many florets open or one carrying few open flowers. Flowers that are irregularly spaced or so placed that the stem is visible between them. Flowers that are small for the cultivar, of poor form, texture or colour.

Advice to judges Removal of florets should be discouraged. However, if removal adds to the overall balance and pleasing appearance of the spike, up to two florets may be removed but preference will be given to complete spikes. The removal of more than two florets is a major fault. Colour preference should not be taken into account.

Condition	6 points
Length and form of spike	6 points
Size, form and texture of flowers for the cultivar)	4 points
Colour	4 points
TOTAL	20 points

Gladiolus, primulinus type

Merits An erect spike, with fresh unblemished blooms and foliage. Stem slender but strong, carrying 14 to 20 flowers and buds. Flowers are regularly and gracefully placed in a stepladder arrangement, facing forwards with one upper petal hooding over the centre, the whole presenting a light appearance.

Defects A bent, twisted spike, heavy stem or with blemished foliage. Flowers tightly placed so as to hide the stem, not facing forward and without a hooded upper inside petal. Flowers not typical of the cultivar and heavy in general appearance.

Advice to judges Removal of florets should be discouraged. However, if removal adds to the overall balance and pleasing appearance of the spike, up to two florets may be removed but preference will be given to complete spikes. The removal of more than two florets is a major fault. Colour preference should not be taken into account.

Condition	4 points
Length and form of spike	6 points
Size, form and texture of flowers for the cultivar)	6 points
Colour	4 points
TOTAL	20 points

Gourds, ornamental

Most gourds are small fruited, of various colours and colour patterns, warted or with other bulges. A number of fruits will be required to demonstrate a range of the possibilities. The fruit should be displayed for effect on a dish or in a basket, to present a well-balanced and attractive display. Ornamental gourds must not be included in vegetable classes.

Merits Fresh, fully developed, mature fruits with stalks attached, unvarnished, showing variation in colour and form and presenting a uniform mixture.

Defects Misshapen, immature, old, diseased or damaged fruit. Lack of stalk or uniformity.

Advice to Judges Although gourds are vegetables, more than one cultivar may be shown on a dish.

Condition	4 points
Size, form and shape	4 points
Colour	4 points
TOTAL	12 points

Heathers

Merits Good condition. Long, straight spikes of evenly spaced florets or large umbels with florets symmetrically arranged. Few unopened buds. No faded florets. Corollas undamaged. Foliage clean, bright-coloured and healthy.

Defects Unsatisfactory condition. Spikes that are short, crooked or uneven, or thinly or irregularly furnished with flowers. Buds not yet open. Florets fading or turning brown. Corollas pierced by insects. Foliage that is dull, withered or unhealthy.

Condition	6 points
Spikes	6 points
Colour	4 points
Uniformity	4 points
TOTAL	20 points

Irises

The following is a general guide to judging iris classes. More detailed information about the many iris categories and guidelines for judging them can be obtained from the British Iris Society (www.britishirissociety.org.uk).

Merits Stems that are sturdy. Well-proportioned, fresh flowers of good colour. Clean foliage.

Defects Stems that are weak. Flowers that are damaged, unhealthy or fading. Blemished foliage.

Condition, including the number of flowers open at the time of judging	5 points
Colour	5 points
Stem and foliage	5 points
Quality of flower	5 points
TOTAL	20 points

Orchids

The following paragraphs were prepared in consultation with the British Orchid Council (BOC; www.british-orchid-council.info). For specialist shows, BOC rules may apply in place of those outlined below.

Merits Flowers complete, of good shape, balance and clear colour or combination of colours for the genus, good contrast and markings. Number of flowers on spike appropriate to or more than expected for genus. Free from pest and disease damage. Pseudobulbs of good quality. Plants well presented with a good number of growths, new leads and spikes.

Defects A smaller than expected plant with poor growth, damage to leaves and too few spikes. A high proportion of the flowers not fully open or over with fading or poor colour. A low total number of flowers, spikes that are kinked or have been disbudded. Evidence of pest or disease damage.

Plant size and condition	8 points
Number of spikes, flowers and presentation	7 points
Flower form	3 points
Flower colour	3 points
Flower size	3 points
Flower substance	2 points
Floriferousness of spike and spike habit	4 points
Total	30 points

Pansies, fancy (exhibition cultivars)

(See also **Violas**, p171)

Merits A flower that is large, fresh, clean, circular in outline, with smooth, thick, velvety petals without serrations, lying evenly on each other and either flat or slightly reflexed so that the surface of the flower is slightly convex. Centre petals that meet above the eye and reach well up on the top petals and a bottom petal that is sufficiently deep and broad to balance the others. Colours that are harmonious; belting (margin) of uniform width; blotches that are large, solid, rounded and clearly defined; and an eye that is bright yellow, solid, circular and well defined.

Defects   A flower that is small, is over, blemished or damaged, concave or lacking a circular outline. Petals that are fishtailed, thin, of poor substance or serrated. Belting (margin) that is too narrow or too broad, or of uneven width or ill-defined; blotches that are small, thin or ragged-edged; an eye that is dull or ill-defined.

Condition	3 points
Form and texture	5 points
Size	3 points
Colour	3 points
Belting	2 points
Blotch	2 points
Eye	2 points
TOTAL	20 points

Pansies, fancy (garden cultivars)

(See also **Violas**, p171)

Judging characteristics for this group should closely follow those for the exhibition cultivars. However, it should be noted that as garden cultivars are generally raised from seed each year, there will be a greater degree of variation than found among the exhibition types, named cultivars of which are reproduced vegetatively.

Merits   A flower that is large, clean and fresh. Uniformity in the size, form and symmetry of markings (blotch and margins), though these may differ in their proportions compared with what is expected of an exhibition cultivar.

Defects   A flower that is small, is over, blemished or damaged, concave or lacking a circular outline. Petals of poor substance, a blotch that is lacking density or ill-defined edges. A V-shaped gap between the middle petals. The top edge of the bottom petal sloping sharply downwards. An ill-defined eye that runs into the blotch.

Points   As for **Pansies, fancy (exhibition cultivars)**, p158.

Pansies, show

(See also **Violas**, p171)

Merits   A flower that is between 38mm and 50mm in diameter, fresh and clean and with the same form, texture and eye as in a fancy pansy. A bicolour flower with a ground-colour of the same shade throughout, circular, broad, of uniform width and well defined at its edge. Belting (margin) of uniform width, of exactly the same colour as the top petals, distinct from the ground-colour and well defined at its junction with the ground-colour. A blotch of good size (though smaller than in a fancy pansy), dense, solid and approximately circular.

In a "dark self-coloured" flower: the same shade throughout with no trace of a blotch. In any other "self-coloured" flower: the same shade throughout except for a blotch as in a bicolour.

Defects A flower that is less than 38mm or wider than 50mm in diameter, past its best, soil marked, concave or lacking a circular outline. Petals that are fishtailed, thin or of poor substance or serrated. Belting (margin) that is very narrow or very wide, of uneven width or ill-defined or not of the same colour as the top petals or not distinct from the ground-colour. Except in a "dark self-coloured" flower, a blotch that is small, thin or ragged-edged. An eye that is dull or ill-defined.

Points *As for Pansies, fancy (exhibition cultivars), p158.*

Pelargoniums, ivy-leaved

Merits A floriferous plant of pleasing form. Ample, healthy, clean and bright foliage. Well-developed trusses. A bright, clear and distinct colour.

Defects A plant that is of unpleasing form or is partly defoliated or has insufficient flowers. Leaves that are coarse, yellowing, dull or dirty, or that show evidence of insect injury or disease. Trusses that are not fully developed.

Condition	6 points
Trusses	8 points
Foliage	3 points
Presentation	3 points
TOTAL	20 points

Pelargoniums, zonal and regal

Merits A shapely plant, proportionate to the size of the pot. Trusses should be proportionate in number to the size of the plant and of bright, clear and distinct colour. Large, round flowers (pips) with broad overlapping petals.

Defects A misshapen or partly defoliated plant, with too few trusses for its size. Trusses that are small, thin, or have too few fully expanded flowers (pips) or have weak stems. Leaves that are coarse, yellowing or dirty, or that show evidence of insect injury or disease.

Condition	6 points
Trusses	8 points
Foliage	3 points

Presentation	3 points
TOTAL	20 points

Pinks

Singles: must have five evenly shaped flat petals at right angles to the stem, or five evenly shaped, waved petals which need not be at right angles to the stem. In both cases the petals should overlap.
Doubles: consist of all other pinks that are not single, irrespective of the number of petals.

Pinks may be classed according to colour as follows:
"Selfs", which must be of one clear colour.
Bi-colours, which must have two colours in concentric zones on every petal; the boundary between the colours should be clear.
Fancies, which may have any ground-colour and be marked or suffused with another contrasting colour or colours on every petal.
Laced Pinks, which may be double, or single with five petals, with unbroken laced markings on every petal.

Merits Good condition. Flowers that are symmetrical, circular in outline and appear light and dainty. Petals that are of good substance, flat and with edges either smooth or regularly serrated. Guard-petals broad and at right angles to the calyx. In double pinks, inner petals that are evenly disposed, diminishing in size toward the centre. Calyx not split. Stems that are rigid, supporting the flowers so that they face upward or at a slight angle, and carrying subsidiary blooms or buds. Clear, bright, colours and well-defined markings, if any. A strong scent. Glaucous foliage. Uniformity.

Defects Unsatisfactory condition. Flowers that are asymmetrical, not circular in outline, or appearing coarse. Petals that are of poor substance or ribbed. Guard-petals that are narrow or are incurved or recurved. Inner petals of double pinks that are not evenly disposed. Calyx split. Stems not rigid, with flowers that face downward, or that carry no subsidiary blooms or buds. Poor colours or ill-defined markings. Lack of fragrance. Lack of uniformity. Unless specifically permitted by the schedule, exhibits with supports to the stems or calyx-bands should be disqualified.

Condition	6 points
Form	6 points
Colour	3 points
Size (for cultivar)	3 points
Presentation	2 points
TOTAL	20 points

Polyanthus

Merits Good condition, including healthy, undamaged foliage and flowers. Long, stout, erect flower stems. Large, compact, symmetrical trusses. Large, circular, flat pips of good substance. Bright colours.

Defects A plant in poor condition or with unhealthy or damaged foliage or flowers. Flower stems that are short, weak or not erect. Trusses that are small or loose or have such short pedicels that the pips overlap unduly. Pips that are small, starry, not flat or of poor substance.

Advice to Judges The above guidelines apply to flowers. For cut flowers *see Flowers from annual, biennial, bulbous and herbaceous plants, p131)*

Condition	5 points
Flower stems	4 points
Trusses	4 points
Pips	4 points
Colour	3 points
TOTAL	20 points

Pot plants and house plants
(other than those for which separate criteria are given elsewhere in this section)

Pots or containers should be clean and undamaged and where staking, tying or wiring is necessary, it should be neatly done in a manner that does not detract from the appearance of the plant. The pot should be in proportion to the plant.

Ferns, bromeliads and orchids and similar plants that are naturally epiphytic may be shown attached to a piece of bark or wood instead of in pots and should not be disqualified in a pot-plant class simply because they are not shown with their roots inside a container.

Judges must consider only the attribute called for in the wording of the class and, if they are judging a foliage class, must take no account of any flowers on a plant, while, when judging a flowering-plant class, they must only award points for foliage on the usual scale. For show purposes the highly coloured ornamental bracts on plants such as *Bougainvillea*, *Euphorbia* (poinsettia) and *Justicia* (*Beloperone*) are considered to be an integral part of the flower and do not qualify for consideration as foliage in pot plant classes.

Where it is usual to grow a number of corms, tubers, cuttings or bulbs in a pot to give a well-furnished appearance (*eg Achimenes*, *Tradescantia* or *Freesia*) the pot is admissible as "a pot plant" even though there is more than one plant in the container.

Flowering or fruiting plants
Merits A sturdy, shapely plant, well furnished with healthy,

unblemished foliage and flowers, displaying flowers, coloured bracts or fruits of good size, colour and substance. Preference should be given to decorative rather than botanical value.

Defects A drawn, undernourished plant with unhealthy, deformed, undersized, scanty or diseased foliage and flowers with undersized flowers, bracts or fruits of poor substance and dull, ill-defined colours.

Advice to judges Most flowering and fruiting pot plants should be shown for all-round effect but others, such as orchids and large-flowered begonias, should not be downpointed for this reason. Difficulty of cultivation may be taken into account.

Condition	6 points
Quality and quantity of bloom or fruit	6 points
Cultivation	5 points
Difficulty of cultivation	3 points
TOTAL	20 points

Foliage plants (decorative in form and/or colour)

Merits A sturdy, shapely plant, well furnished with clean, unblemished, healthy foliage. Preference should be given to decorative rather than botanical value.

Defects A drawn, undernourished plant with unhealthy, deformed, undersized, scanty or diseased foliage, of little ornamental value.

Advice to judges The presence of flowers on a foliage plant should not be considered a fault but the decorative value of the flowers should be disregarded. Most foliage pot plants should be shown for all-round effect. Difficulty of cultivation may be taken into account.

Condition	6 points
Decorative value	6 points
Cultivation	5 points
Difficulty of cultivation	3 points
TOTAL	20 points

Primroses

Merits A tufted and compact habit of growth. Foliage and flowers that are healthy and undamaged. Numerous flowers, produced singly on long peduncles and forming a symmetrical mass. Flowers of good substance, circular in outline with definite, clear colours.

Defects A plant with a loose habit of growth or with unhealthy or blemished foliage or flowers. Flowers that are few or have short stalks or are not arranged symmetrically or are of poor substance or are not circular in outline.

Condition	6 points
Floriferousness	5 points
Flowers	6 points
Colour	3 points
TOTAL	20 points

Primula species including *P. malacoides*, *P. obconica* and *P. sinensis* types

Merits   A vigorous, undamaged and unblemished plant which has numerous open flowers. Trusses with strong stems, carrying the flowers well above the foliage. Flowers well formed, of good substance and with fresh, clear colours.

Defects   A plant that is drawn or weak or has damaged or blemished foliage or few flowers or is ill-balanced. Trusses that are small or that do not carry the flowers above the foliage. Flowers that are of poor substance.

Condition	6 points
Trusses	5 points
Flowers	6 points
Colour	3 points
TOTAL	20 points

Rock-garden plants
See Alpine-house and rock-garden plants, p132

Roses, general
The following paragraphs summarise the Royal National Rose Society (RNRS) rules and were prepared in consultation with the RNRS (www.rnrs.org.uk).

Notes

Large-flowered (HT), cluster-flowered: for exhibition purposes the expressions 'large flowered' and 'cluster flowered' apply wherever appropriate to all divisions of modern garden roses, not just modern repeat-flowering bush roses. Whatever the type, the exhibit must meet the standards applicable to the class in which the exhibit is entered.

Stem: an original new growth with no lateral growth present and one that has not been 'stopped'. Stems with lateral growth removed should not be downpointed. Stems with lateral growth present, or where growth has been stopped, should be downpointed by 3 points per stem. Disbudding and deadheading are permitted under this rule.

Double blooms: blooms with more than 20 petals.

Semi-double blooms: blooms with between eight and 20 petals.

Single blooms: blooms with less than eight petals.

Side buds: these are permitted in all large-flowered classes except those for Specimen Blooms and for Three Stage Roses. No more than 3 buds/sprays per stem are permitted under this rule.

Foliage: unless expressly permitted by the schedule, the insertion of any additional foliage disqualifies an exhibit. The 'dressing' of foliage by the use of anything other than plain water is not permitted.

Wiring: a single wire may be used to hold the flowerhead erect, but only with large-flowered roses. Untidy wiring must be downpointed.

Merits
- **Individual bloom:** double blooms in the 'perfect stage' should be half to three-quarters open with the petals symmetrically arranged within a circular outline.

  For any large-flowered (HT) type, the outer petals should regularly surround an upright and well-formed conical and pointed centre. For any other type the outer petals should regularly surround a central formation typical of the cultivar, *eg* rounded, rosette, quartered, pompon, etc.

  Double blooms in the 'full bloom' stage should be fully open with the petals symmetrically arranged within a circular outline; the stamens, if exposed, should be fresh and of good colour.

  Single and semi-double blooms in the 'perfect' or 'full bloom' stage (often indistinguishable) should have petals that are symmetrically arranged within a circular outline and the stamens, if exposed, should be fresh and of good colour.

  Any type in the 'bud stage' should show full colour with one or two petals beginning to unfurl above an opening calyx.

  Any type in the 'hip stage' should have fruit that is fully developed and of the typical size, shape and colour of a ripe hip of the cultivar.
- **Cluster:** two or more blooms. The inflorescence should be representative of its cultivar with the blooms gracefully arranged and so spaced as to permit their natural development, neither being crushed together nor exposing wide gaps between them. **Note:** this does not apply to large-flowered roses.
- **Substance:** this refers to the petals, which should be firm, smooth and of good texture, neither coarse nor flimsy and free from blemish.
- **Size of individual bloom:** the bloom should be of good average size for a well-grown plant of the particular cultivar. Except in classes for 'specimen blooms', where size is important irrespective of cultivar, a bloom of above-average size should not be regarded as being of special merit.
- **Freshness of bloom:** appearance should be sparkling and clean with no suggestion of tiredness, staleness or unnatural preservation.
- **Brilliance of colour:** the colour should be bright and glowing, not dull or faded.
- **Purity of colour:** the bloom should display the full depth of the true seasonal colour of the cultivar, with no suggestion of deviation, blueing or tarnishing.
- **Stem:** the stem should be straight and proportionate in thickness and length to the size of the bloom it supports, being neither unduly thin and spindly nor coarsely thick and clumsy.
- **Foliage:** adequate in quantity and size; undamaged, fresh and clean

in appearance, of good colour and substance for the cultivar and with no evidence of the use of artificial aids to enhance appearance.
Note: stem and foliage standards are not applied when judging 'specimen blooms' in boxes.

• **Presentation:** the exhibit should be balanced in height and width in relation to the container, and enhanced by good colour combination. The flowers and foliage should be artistically arranged to avoid either crushing or excessive gaps and without exposing such expanses of stem or foliage that the flowers are not the dominant feature of the exhibit. In exhibits comprising numbers of individual blooms (typically boxes, bowls, palettes or vases of specimen and miniature roses) the blooms should be uniform in size, state of development and freshness. The overall shape of basket exhibits should follow the contours of the basket and permit the theoretical use of the handle.

• **Roses grown and staged in pots or other containers:** it is important to note the difference between 'a rose grown in a pot or container' and 'a pot or container of roses'. In the former, only one plant is required while in the latter a number of plants is permissible. The plants should be representative of well-grown specimens of the cultivar and present a well-balanced exhibit.

Defects

Individual blooms of irregular outline; having fewer than average number of petals; split, blunt or confused centres; stained or damaged petals; evidence of removal or trimming of petals; immaturity or over-development of blooms; over-dressing so as to appear unnatural; blooms left tied or with pellets of cotton wool.

Clusters with poor outline, blooms irregularly placed; crushed tightly together or so widely spaced as to show gaps; a high proportion of unopened buds or aged blooms; hips or stalks of spent blooms left showing.

Poor substance of petals; flimsy and drooping or rough, coarse, creased or diseased.

Size not representative of a well-grown example of the cultivar.

Blooms that do not appear to be sparkling fresh; giving an impression of being tired, drawn, stale or wan.

Dull or faded colour. Deviation from true colour of a well-grown example of the cultivar, excessive white streaking, dark or tarnished markings, blueing (especially of red roses.)

Stems weak, twisted, bent, flattened in section, unduly thick in relation to the blooms carried, marked, diseased or damaged.

Poor, thin foliage, inadequate in size or quantity; of bad colour, misshapen, misplaced, diseased or damaged.

Untidy presentation; unpleasant overall effect, lopsided appearance, obtrusive wiring (where wiring is permitted), excessive or inadequate length of stem in relation to the size and number of blooms carried; exhibit too tall and narrow or too flat and wide;

flowers or clusters crushed together or too widely spaced; poor colour balance; excessive display of stems and/or foliage so that the flowers are not the dominant feature of the exhibit; dirty containers or boxes.

Roses, except specimen blooms, three-stage roses and miniature roses

Merits   As for *Roses, general*
Defects   As for *Roses, general*
Advice to judges   Each receptacle is considered as a separate unit. Thus, in a class for one vase or bowl, 20 points is the maximum possible score; while in a class for three vases, each vase is assessed out of 20 points so that 60 points is the maximum possible score for an exhibit.

In classes that specify a minimum and/or maximum number of cultivars, blooms or stems, the number actually staged may be taken into consideration as an additional criterion (excluding any stems that have been downpointed). If blooms are left tied or with pellets of cotton wool, up to 3 points must be deducted for each bloom so left in each receptacle. Blooms so overdressed as to alter their character must be regarded as very seriously defective and must be downpointed.

Form and size of individual bloom(s), form of cluster(s), substance	5 points
Freshness, brilliance, purity of colour	5 points
Stems and foliage	3 points
Presentation	7 points
TOTAL	20 points

Roses, specimen blooms in bowls, vases and baskets with stems and foliage

Merits   As for *Roses, general*, except the merit for cluster which does not apply.
Defects   As for *Roses, general*, except the defect for cluster which does not apply.
Advice to judges   In awarding points each receptacle is considered as a separate unit. Thus, in a class for one vase or bowl, 20 points is the maximum possible score while in a class for three vases, each vase is assessed out of 20 points so that 60 points is the maximum score for the exhibit.

In classes that specify a minimum and/or maximum number of cultivars or stems, the number actually staged should also be taken into consideration as an additional criterion (excluding any stems that have been downpointed). If blooms are left tied or with pellets of cotton wool, up to 3 points must be deducted for each bloom so left. Blooms so overdressed as to alter their character must be regarded as very seriously defective and must be downpointed.

Form and size of individual bloom(s), form of cluster(s), substance	5 points
Freshness, brilliance, purity of colour	5 points
Stems and foliage	3 points
Presentation	7 points
TOTAL	20 points

Roses, specimen blooms in boxes, palettes, picture frames, glass dishes, glass bowls

These are not commonly seen at flower shows. Refer to the RNRS for detailed guidance.

Three-stage roses, including large-flowered, miniature and miniflora roses

Three blooms of one cultivar: one in the bud stage, one in the perfect stage, and one in the full bloom stage (refer to **Roses, General, Notes** for further details of these stages).

Merits As for **Roses, general**

Defects As for **Roses, general**

Advice to judges The bud should be showing its full colour, with one or two petals beginning to unfurl above an opening calyx. The perfect-stage bloom should be of average size for the cultivar, half to three-quarters open with the petals symmetrically arranged within a circular outline. The full bloom should be of average size for the cultivar and should be fully open with the petals arranged within a circular outline; the stamens, if exposed, should be fresh and of a good colour. Each stem must be of the same cultivar. If blooms are left tied or with pellets of cotton wool, up to 3 points must be deducted for each bloom so left in each receptacle. Blooms so overdressed as to alter their character must be regarded as very seriously defective and must be downpointed.

Form and size of individual blooms, substance	5 points
Freshness, brilliance, purity of colour	5 points
Stems and foliage	3 points
Presentation	7 points
TOTAL	20 points

Miniature roses in bowls, baskets and vases

Merits As for **Roses, general**. In addition, miniature roses should be miniature in all aspects of size of flowers, foliage and stems. All types of miniature roses are eligible but they must be representative of their cultivar and conform to the requirements of the schedule. Foliage should be representative of the cultivar and in reasonable proportion to the size of the blooms. In classes for bowls, baskets and vases, the exhibit must be balanced in relation to the container and arranged and spaced so as to permit the natural development of the blooms, neither being crushed together nor exposing wide gaps between stems or individual blooms. All exhibits should be presented with an emphasis on the daintiness appropriate to miniature roses.

Defects As for *Roses, general*

Advice to judges In awarding points, each receptacle is considered as a separate unit. Thus, in a class for one vase or bowl, 20 points is the maximum possible score while, in a class for three vases, each vase is assessed out of 20 points so that 60 points is the maximum possible score for an exhibit.

In classes that specify a minimum and/or maximum number of cultivars, blooms or stems, the number actually staged may be taken into consideration as an additional criterion (excluding any stems that have been downpointed). If blooms are left tied or with pellets of cotton wool, up to 3 points must be deducted for each bloom so left in each receptacle. Blooms so overdressed as to alter their character must be regarded as very seriously defective and must be downpointed.

Form and size of individual bloom(s), form of cluster(s), substance and stage of development	5 points
Freshness, brilliance, purity of colour	5 points
Stems and foliage	3 points
Presentation	7 points
TOTAL	**20 points**

Miniature roses in boxes, palettes, picture frames, glass dishes and collage bowls

These are not commonly seen at local flower shows. Refer to the RNRS for detailed guidance.

Three-stage miniature roses

See Three-stage roses, p168

Sweet peas

Merits Strong spikes with well-spaced blooms, each one fully open and fresh. Large flowers with erect standards, rigid wings and keel closed, free from colour-running, spotting or scorching and of a bright colour with a silken sheen. Long, straight stems in proportion to the size of the blooms. Effectiveness of staging (particularly when competition is close).

Defects Weak spikes with irregularly placed blooms or having undeveloped or poorly coloured top blooms or with blooms showing seed pods or losing colour. Flowers small for the cultivar, malformed, spotted, scorched or with poor or running colour. Stems crooked or disproportionately short or long for the size of the blooms. Stems with fewer than four flowers.

Advice to Judges Ensure that both the top and bottom blooms are of similar condition and size and that each stem is evenly spaced.

Freshness, cleanliness and condition	7 points
Form, placement and uniformity	6 points
Trueness of colour	4 points
Size of bloom in balance with stem	3 points
TOTAL	20 points

Tulips

All tulips with the exception of those in the Single and Late Double and Parrot Groups must have six petals and six filaments with anthers. Any exhibit containing flowers that have more or less than this number would not be disqualified, but would only receive an award in the absence of acceptable exhibits. Any exhibit containing flowers that are clearly diseased as a result of *Tulip breaking virus* will not be considered for an award. No artificial support or wiring of blooms is allowed.

Merits Flowers in good condition, in their most perfect phase and unblemished, of a good colour for the cultivar, of firm substance and smooth texture and of the form typical of the group to which the cultivar belongs. Stems that are stiff and strong enough to support the flowers, with attached foliage that is stiff and in good condition.

Defects Flowers immature or past their perfect phase, spotted, blistered or otherwise blemished, of poor colour for the cultivar, thin, of rough texture or not of the form typical of their group. Stems limp or too weak to support the flowers, with foliage that is limp or very badly blemished.

Advice to judges Where there are a number of flowers in a vase then uniformity of size and form is very important and a maximum of 5 additional points should be awarded in a class calling for three to six blooms, and a maximum of 10 points for nine to 18 blooms. Flowers of tulips in the Viridiflora Group will have green markings and this is not a fault.

Condition	4 points
Form	4 points
Colour	4 points
Size (for the cultivar)	2 points
Substance	3 points

Stems and attached foliage	3 points
TOTAL	20 points

Violas (exhibition cultivars)

(See also **Pansies, fancy** (**exhibition cultivars**), pp158–159)

Merits A flower that is large, fresh, clean and of the form, build and texture outlined for fancy pansies (see pp158–159). While the colour may be self, striped, mottled, suffused or belted (margined), there must be no semblance of a blotch or any rays and the eye must be bright, solid, circular and well defined.

Defects A flower that is less than 63mm in diameter, past its best, marked or damaged, concave or lacking a circular outline. Petals fishtailed or with V-shaped gaps between them or thin, of poor substance or serrated. Any semblance of a blotch or of rays. An eye that is very large or is square or ill-defined.

Condition	3 points
Form and texture	5 points
Size	3 points
Colour	7 points
Eye	2 points
TOTAL	20 points

Violas (garden cultivars)

(See also **Pansies**, pp158–159)

Merits A flower that is clean, fresh and of good substance. Circular or oval in form without trace of blotch or ray. An eye that is well defined, circular and a bright yellow or orange. "Selfs" have a clear and distinct ground colour. Margined flowers have well-defined edges of contrasting colour. Fancy, striped or suffused flowers show a pleasing or striking contrast.

Defects A flower that is less than 25mm or wider than 50mm in diameter, past its best, marked or damaged, lacking a circular or oval form. Petals of poor substance with dull or faded colour. Any semblance of blotch or ray, or gaps between petals. A large or square eye that runs into the ground colour.

Points As for **Violas** (**exhibition cultivars**), above.

JUDGING GARDENS AND ALLOTMENTS

The inspection of gardens and allotments in competition with each other should be timed so that an assessment of the ornamental or productive value may be made rather than simply judging the entry at its peak. This will normally require the judges to make at least two visits, one in June or the first week in July and another between mid-August and mid-September. Where possible all entries in the competition should be assessed within a maximum period of five days.

Competitors should be given an indication of when their garden or allotment is likely to be visited.

Competition organisers should ensure that the judge is accompanied by a steward who knows the exact location of all the entrants and has copies of their official entries.

1 The judging of gardens

Domestic gardens fall within three broad categories.

Amenity gardens with less than 20 percent devoted to the production of fruit and/or vegetables.

Dual-purpose gardens with between 20 and 50 percent devoted to the production of fruit and/or vegetables as well as a substantial amenity area.

Utility gardens in which more than 50 percent is devoted to the production of fruit and/or vegetables and only a small space reserved for amenity or ornamental purposes.

In the judging of gardens credit should be given to the best use of the space, the quality of the plants including grassed areas, design and the placing of plants in suitable locations and aspects.

The overall size of the garden should not be taken into account nor should the diversity or lack of diversity of plants. A limited number of healthy, well-grown plants making the best use of the space available is more meritorious than a wide variety of plants poorly grown and overcrowded or sparsely planted.

Brown patches in lawns where the spent foliage of spring bulbs such as daffodils or crocuses has recently been mown off must not be considered a demerit. The relative immaturity of some trees or shrubs should not, in itself, be considered a fault provided that the plant is appropriately sited and, where necessary, properly staked and/or protected.

Judging gardens and alliotments

The following pointing systems are offered as a guide.

Amenity gardens

Health, vigour and suitability of plants	100 points
Suitability of design to its site and usage	75 points
Maintenance of paths, structures, lawns and other grassed areas and working areas	50 points
Cultivation and freedom from perennial weeds	50 points
Harmonious blending of colours, shapes and textures	75 points
TOTAL	**350 points**

Dual-purpose gardens

Health, vigour and suitability of plants in both amenity and kitchen garden areas	100 points
Maintenance of paths, structures, lawns and grassed areas and working areas	50 points
Range and cultivation of plants in the kitchen garden area	75 points
Design and co-ordination of colours, shapes and textures in the amenity area	75 points
Overall integration of the two elements into a single, attractive, practical whole	50 points
TOTAL	**350 points**

Utility gardens

Health, vigour, cultivation and arrangement of vegetables, and/or flowers, and/or fruit and/or culinary herb crops	125 points
Planning for regular rotations, and successional plantings to give optimum use of space, year-round produce and to minimise the build-up of pests and soil borne diseases	75 points
Maintenance of paths, crops, supports, cloches, frames and other structures	50 points
Utilisation of boundary walls or fences or other supports for training soft or top fruits or climbing vegetables	50 points
Neatness, practicality, planting and design of amenity area and the suitability of its siting within the overall garden area	50 points
TOTAL	**350 points**

(1 The judging of gardens continued)

Alternatively the following pointing system may be used:

Vegetable gardens

Section 1 Cultivation (cropping scheme, quality of work, cleanliness, stored humus or compost heap)	25 points
Section 2 For potatoes, 12; winter brassicas, 12; onions, 12; carrots, 12; celery, 8; leeks, 8; beetroot, 6; parsnips, 5	75 points
Section 3 For peas, 12; runner or climbing beans, 12; summer brassicas, 12; lettuces, 8; tomatoes, 8; broad beans, 6; dwarf French beans, 6; vegetable marrows, 6	70 points
Section 4 For any other kinds of vegetable not mentioned above (including salads), 5 points each kind; not more than six kinds to receive points in final total.	30 points
TOTAL	**200 points**

Flower gardens

Section 1 For general scheme, 30; tasteful arrangement, 20; cultivation and cleanliness, 20	70 points
Section 2 For shrubs and trees, climbers, rock garden, lawn, paths, greenhouse, fences and hedges: 8 each, but only four of these to receive marks	32 points
Section 3 For hardy herbaceous perennials, annuals and biennials, roses, tender plants, windowboxes, window plants, etc: 8 each, but only four of these to receive marks.	32 points
Section 4 For special features	16 points
TOTAL	**150 points**

Glasshouses, frames and other protected areas

Section 1 Standard of cultivation, 15; utilisation of growing space, 10; cleanliness, 5	30 points
Section 2 For tomatoes, 10; cucumbers, 10; aubergines, 10; peppers, 10; fruit, 10; but only three of these to receive marks.	30 points
Section 3 Ornamental pot plants	20 points
Section 4 Other plants, 5; specialist collections, 15	20 points
TOTAL	**100 points**

Judging gardens and alliotments

Fruit gardens
The garden should contain not less than six kinds of fruits.
Section 1 For the overall planting scheme 20;
  good pruning, training, tree and bush form
  and plant supports 20; cultivation, cleanliness,
  pest and disease control 18   58 points
Section 2 For apples, 12; pears, 10; plums, 10;
  grapes, 10; cherries, 8; currants, black, 8;
  currants, other than black, 8; gooseberries, 8;
  raspberries, 8; strawberries, 8; blackberries,
  or hybrid berries, 8   98 points
(The tree and bush fruits to consist of at least two plants of any one kind, grapes one, blackberries and/or hybrid berries two, strawberries 4m of row and raspberries 4m length of row.)

Section 3 For peach and/or nectarine fan trained, 10;
  in bush form, 8; fig fan trained, 10   28 points
Section 4 For any other kind of fruit not mentioned
  above 4 points each kind, not more than four kinds
  to receive points in final total.   16 points
TOTAL   200 points

2 The judging of allotments

For competition purposes an allotment is considered to be an area of land separate from and in addition to the household garden adjacent to the owner's property; or a plot cultivated by a householder who has no garden as part of his/her own domestic premises.

The primary purpose of an allotment is to provide crops of vegetables, fruit, flowers and culinary herbs for household use and the more completely a plot fulfils this objective the greater should be the credit accorded to it in competition.

Allotments also allow enthusiasts for one particular plant or group of plants to indulge their particular passion and a plot given over to the monoculture of, for example, dahlias or carnations must be judged according to the standard and quality of cultivation.

The size of plot should not be a factor for consideration in competition but where there are a great many entries of varying sizes organisers should consider dividing the competition into three or four separate classes according to size.

(2 The judging of allotments continued)

The following pointing systems are offered as a guide but competition organisers may wish to adapt these to suit local conditions or requirements.

Condition of the plot   60 points
Plots should be well stocked with crops free from obvious signs of excessive damage by pests, disease or weather. Any unplanted areas where crops have just been harvested or that are about to be planted up should be clean and free from weeds and the soil should be of a good, well cultivated condition and texture.

Good workmanship   50 points
Soil between the crops should contain little or no evidence of weeds. Paths and leisure areas where included should be neatly edged, even and well maintained. Evidence of planting for a constant succession of crops should be given credit. Intelligent use of organic methods of pest control such as the pinching out of broad bean tips to inhibit blackfly or the use of barriers against carrot root fly should be given credit. Supports for those plants that require them should be properly positioned and sturdy enough to withstand bad weather.

Quality of crops, flowers, fruit and vegetables
    and plants   150 points
All plants should be vigorous, sturdy and free from obvious signs of excessive damage by pests, disease or weather. A broad range of food crops, both vegetables and fruit where the latter is permitted, should be in cultivation and flowers grown for cutting or decoration should be assessed on the same basis as the food crops ie with a regard to their health, skill in cultivation and suitability to the site. The inclusion of culinary herbs in the cropping scheme should be considered meritorious.

Originality of layout and planting   25 points
The intelligent adaptation of the layout to suit the needs of the plot-holder, the use of companion planting to reduce damage by pests and a pleasing overall visual effect should be considered meritorious. The cultivation of less common crops and the use of no-dig or deep-bed methods of cultivation should be given credit.

Ingenuity in overcoming local problems   25 points
Plot-holders who have overcome difficulties such as oddly shaped sites, difficult soil conditions, exposed aspect or excessive shading and dehydration by an adjacent tree belt should be given credit for raising an acceptable (ie usable) standard of crop.

Judging gardens and alliotments

Visual aspect of the plot   **20 points**
The overall appearance of the plot should be neat and pleasing and the balance of the cultivation, as far as is allowed by local regulations, should be as broad as possible.

Condition of garden sheds, etc   **20 points**
Sheds, if present, should be of a neat and workmanlike appearance both inside and out. Frames, cloches and greenhouses should be clean and well maintained. Pea and bean supports should be sturdy enough for the weight of the crops that they bear and any bird netting should be properly positioned and undamaged so as to afford protection to the crops over which they have been placed.

TOTAL   **350 points**

JUDGING HANGING BASKETS AND CONTAINERS

These classes require a colourful, harmonious display of plants in as perfect a condition as possible.

Plants should be closely grouped and overflow the edges of their container so as to hide or almost hide it. They should be arranged in an attractive, well-balanced fashion and must be healthy and well developed with no obvious signs of damage.

The flowers and foliage should blend with each other and their container. The use of a single colour or one single type of plant is acceptable provided the plants are well grown and attractively presented. Containers that use or include fruits or vegetables such as alpine strawberries, cherry tomatoes or non-hearting lettuce should be assessed on the same basis as those using flowering or foliage plants.

For those who require one, a pointing system is suggested as follows:

Quality, health, vigour and appropriateness of planting	100 points
Initial impact of colours, and/or textures	50 points
Presentation, balance and symmetry of display	50 points
TOTAL	200 points

Judging hanging baskets and containers

GLOSSARY

Alpine   Loosely applied to any plant that is suitable for a rock garden or alpine house.

Amateur   A person who, not being a professional either personally or with unpaid or paid assistance, maintains a garden or grows plants, flowers, fruit or vegetables for pleasure and enjoyment and not for a livelihood. (It is permissible for an amateur to sell surplus fruit and/or vegetables and/or other horticultural produce, provided that the garden is maintained primarily for the pleasure and enjoyment of the household and not as a means of livelihood.)

Annual   A plant that grows from seed and naturally and ordinarily flowers, seeds and dies (irrespective of frost) within twelve months.

Barrel   The shaft or stem of a leek.

Beard   The beard-like growth on the falls of some irises.

Biennial   A plant that grows from seed and ordinarily requires two seasons to complete its life-cycle, growing one year, flowering, seeding and dying in the second.

Blanch   That part of a leek stem which is blanched. In addition, that part of any vegetable that is blanched (*eg* celery, endive).

Blemish   Mark or imperfection on exhibit that may be caused by mechanical damage, physiological deficiency, pest or disease.

Bloom   1 The waxy covering of many fruits and vegetables, *eg* of a plum and a grape, and of the leaves and stems of many succulent and other plants.
2 A bloom: one open flower, *eg* of a tulip, or one flowerhead, *eg* of a chrysanthemum or dahlia (*see also* **Flowerhead**, **Spike** *and* **Spray**).
3 In bloom: bearing at least one open flower (*see p23, paragraph 11*).

Bowl   A vessel for displaying cut flowers in water or for growing bulbous plants and having a mouth-width measurement at least equal to, but usually greater than, its height. In floral arrangement classes, bowls with one or more than one handle are acceptable.

Bract   Usually a small leaf-like structure occurring below the flowers and above the true leaves; sometimes coloured, as in *Euphorbia*.

Bulb   An underground modified stem bearing a number of swollen fleshy leaf bases or scale leaves in which food is stored, the whole enclosing the next year's bud, *eg* the bulb of a daffodil, tulip, hyacinth or onion.

Glossary

Bulbous For horticultural-show purposes "bulbous plants" includes those having bulbs, corms or tubers; "bulbous" may also refer to a defective attribute such as the swelling of a plant, for example, the base of a leek.

Button The point on the barrel of a leek where the lowest leaf breaks the circumference.

Cactus A plant belonging to the family *Cactaceae*, *eg* species of *Cereus*, *Epiphyllum*, *Mammillaria*, *Opuntia* or *Schlumbergera*.

Calyx The outer set of perianth segments, especially when green.

Class A sub-division of a competitive schedule; one group of comparable exhibits.

Collection An assembly of kinds and/or cultivars of plants, flowers, fruits or vegetables in one exhibit.

Conifers Members of the *Coniferae*, which for show purposes includes maidenhair tree (*Ginkgo*).

Container A general term, used particularly in connection with floral arrangements, for bowls, vases and other vessels used to display plants or flowers.

Corm For horticultural-show purposes, a bulb-like swollen underground stem stored with reserve food, *eg Crocus* or *Colchicum*.

Corolla The inner set of perianth segments, if differing from the outer set, and especially if coloured and showy.

Corona A trumpet- or cup-like development of the perianth found in daffodils (*Narcissus*) species and cultivars.

Cultivar The internationally accepted term for what, in English-speaking countries, is commonly known by gardeners as a "cultivated variety" or simply a "variety". (*See **Variety** for the distinction between a cultivar and a botanical variety.*)

Deciduous A deciduous tree or shrub is one having leaves that persist only one season and fall in the autumn.

Dish In horticultural-show schedules, a specified number or quantity of a fruit or vegetable constituting one item that may be displayed on a table or on a stand or on a receptacle of any material and of any shape. Unless permitted by the show schedule, a dish must consist of one cultivar only.

Display   An exhibit in which attractiveness of arrangement and general effect are to be considered of more importance than they would have been had the schedule specified a "group" or a "collection".

Entry   A notification of an intention to exhibit; a unit submitted for exhibition in a competition or show.

Evergreen   A plant that retains its living foliage for at least a full year and is never leafless.

Everlasting   A plant with flowerheads that retain much of their showy character after being cut and dried.

Falls   The three outer segments of an iris flower.

Flags   The leaves of a leek plant.

Florets   Small individual flowers, especially those in heads, as in a chrysanthemum, dahlia or other members of *Asteraceae*.

Flowerhead   For horticultural-show purposes, an assemblage of florets grouped together in a single head on a single flower stem, *eg* a disbudded chrysanthemum or a disbudded dahlia.

Foliage   1 The leaves of any plant.   2 Stems bearing only leaves.

Foliage plant   A plant usually grown for its ornamental foliage. If it is in flower it may be entered into a foliage-plant class but the flowers will not be taken into account.

Forced   Grown to flower or be ready for consumption before the normal time.

Fruits   1 In classes for edible fruits: "fruits" means those normally grown for dessert, either raw or cooked.
2 In classes for ornamental fruits and for floral arrangements: "fruits" means all types of developed ovaries, *eg* seed pods, berries or ornamental gourds.

Genus   A group of related plants having the same generic name, *eg* all species and hybrids of the genus *Lilium*, such as *L. candidum*, *L. chalcedonicum*, *L.* 'Enchantment', *L. henryi* and *L.* × *testaceum*.

Gourds, edible   More usually described as winter squash. *See* **Squash**.
Gourds, ornamental   Edible and inedible fruits of the *Cucurbitaceae*

family. Most are small, of various colours and colour patterns, smooth, warted or with other protuberances. Large specimens can have long necks, *eg* Swan or Dolphin. Used for ornament and in flower arranging, varnished or unvarnished, fresh or dried. Ornamental gourds cannot be shown in vegetable classes.

Grown in the open   1 In classes for fruit, the expression means that the plants or trees have flowered and also set their fruit, as well as ripened it, without any protection beyond netting or a wall-coping not exceeding 600mm in width.
2 In classes for vegetables, for annuals, for plants grown as annuals and for half-hardy ornamental plants, the expression means that the plants have been grown in the ground in the open air without any protection by glass or glass substitute once the danger of spring frosts has passed.
3 In classes for hardy herbaceous plants, trees and shrubs the expression means those grown in the ground in the open air and not with protection by glass or glass substitutes.

Habit   The general appearance or manner of growth of a plant, *eg* compact, straggling, tufted, bushy, shrubby.

Half-hardy   A half-hardy plant is one that may be grown in the open air for part of the year but must be lifted and housed or protected in some other way during winter. In the case of an annual: one that may either be raised under glass and planted out when frosts are no longer feared or sown out of doors in May or early June.

Handle   When referring to judging of cucumbers, this relates to the portion of the fruit closest to the stem. This part will be less in girth than the main body of the fruit and tapering to the stem.

Hardy   A hardy plant is one that is able to survive the average winter when grown in the open without protection.

Herb   For horticultural-show purposes a culinary "herb" is an essential ingredient in many foods, which makes it of value for flavouring soups, stews, sauces, salads, etc. The following are among the more important kinds: angelica, basil, bay, borage, celery leaf, chervil, chives, coriander, dill, fennel, hyssop, lemon balm, lovage, marjoram, mint, oregano, parsley, rocket, rosemary, sage (*Salvia officinalis* only), savory, sorrel, sweet cicely, tarragon and thyme. Seed providers, such as coriander and dill, and root providers, such as Florence fennel, should not be included.

Herbaceous perennial   A plant with a non-woody stem that either dies down to the ground completely each winter, *eg* delphinium, or retains its basal foliage, *eg* bergenia, but which remains alive throughout several years. For show purposes this includes all bulbs, corms, rhizomes and tubers .

Herbaceous plant   A plant that does not form a persistent woody stem. It may be annual, biennial or perennial.

Hilum   The scar on a seed marking the point of attachment to the plant.

House plant   A plant grown for the decorative effect of its foliage, flower or fruit and which, given reasonable treatment, will thrive in a dwelling room for several years. *See pp162–163.*

Hybrid   A plant derived from the intercrossing of two or more genetically distinct plants (in ornamental horticulture, usually two or more species), *eg Lilium × testaceum* is a hybrid resulting from the interbreeding of *L. candidum* and *L. chalcedonicum*; × *Brassocattleya holfordii* is a hybrid resulting from the intercrossing of *Brassavola digbyana* and *Cattleya forbesii*. F_1 hybrids of vegetables and seed-raised flowers are plants raised from seed obtained from crosses between selected parent lines, which themselves can be maintained in the same state over many generations so the hybridization can be repeated many times over a period of years.

Inflorescence   The flowering portion of the stem above the last stem leaves, including its flower branches, bracts and flowers.

Kind   1 A term recommended for use in the classification of fruit and vegetables for show purposes, *eg* apples, grapes, peaches, pears and plums are "kinds" of fruit; asparagus, carrots, onions and peas are "kinds" of vegetable (*see pp66–67 and pp90–93 for lists of different kinds of fruit and vegetables*).
2 When applied to ornamental flowers, "kind" is not a botanical term but has become accepted for show purposes to differentiate between genera. However, the term also applies to annual and perennial forms within the same genera, *eg* annual asters and Michaelmas daisies.
3 Technically, there is no real way in which this type of categorisation can be properly applied to ornamental plants such as annuals, herbaceous plants, trees and shrubs, etc. These plants are all (broadly speaking) either species or cultivars, and those with common characteristics are gathered together in groups called genera which in turn are grouped in families. Thus *Iris danfordiae* and the tall bearded *Iris* 'Grace' are a species and a cultivar of the genus *Iris* which in turn is one of the genera of the family *Iridaceae*. For show purposes, where the object is to attract a wide diversity of plants into a collection

class, it is best to word the schedule to invite "Six hardy herbaceous plants representing at least three genera, one vase of each" or "Four species or cultivars of bulbous plants representing two or more genera, one vase of each" or similar adaptations of these wordings.

Leeks For exhibition purposes leeks are divided into three categories:
1 **Pot**: not more than 150mm from base to button.
2 **Intermediate**: not less than 150mm and not more than 350mm from base to button.
3 **Blanched**: more than 350mm from base to button.

Marrow A nearly full-sized but immature fruit of *Cucurbita pepo*. The skin should be tender. The shape should be cylindrical with blunt ends; traditionally with green stripes but may be other colours.

NAS "not according to schedule" (*see also p61, paragraph 11*).

Natural "Natural", as applied to foliage, flowers or fruits, means as produced by the plant, without any artificial treatment such as dyeing, oiling or varnishing.

Novice A competitor who has not won at a previous show some prize or prizes specified in the definition of a novice in the schedule.

Originality In a schedule "originality" means uncommon or unusual but at the same time desirable.

Panicle For horticultural-show purposes, a branched inflorescence.

Pedicel The stalk of a single flower on an inflorescence (*see also* **Peduncle**).

Peduncle The stalk of an inflorescence or of part of an inflorescence. This term should also be used for a stalk of an inflorescence with a solitary flower (*see also* **Pedicel**).

Perennial A perennial plant is one that lives for more than two years. Perennial plants include trees and shrubs, plants that grow from bulbs, corms, rhizomes and tubers and, in fact, all that are not annuals or biennials. (Antirrhinums, petunias, wallflowers and some other plants are usually grown as annuals or biennials in gardens but, botanically, may be true perennials. In such cases, it is recommended that the horticultural practice of treating them as annuals should be adopted for show purposes to avoid confusion – see p34–35)

Perianth A term used for the calyx and corolla or their equivalents but seldom used except when the segments of the two whorls are both coloured, as in a daffodil or a tulip.

Petal   An individual segment of the corolla, especially one free to the base.

Pip   1 An individual flower of an inflorescence, applied especially to auriculas, delphiniums, gladioli and sweet williams.
2 A bulbil within the inflorescence of leeks, onions and other alliums.
3 The seed within a fruit such as apple or pear.

Pot plant   For horticultural-show purposes, a plant grown in a pot for the decorative effect of its foliage, flower or fruit and for use in a glasshouse or, for a short period, in a dwelling room (*see pp162–163*).

Professional   A person who gains his/her livelihood by growing horticultural plants, flowers, fruit or vegetables for sale or for an employer or anyone employed in the maintenance of a garden, pleasure ground or park.

Pumpkins   Traditionally these are mature fruits ripening to orange and with a hollow seed cavity used for carving into Halloween faces. Principally *Cucurbita pepo* but some large specimens are *C. maxima*, such as 'Mammoth Gourd', 'Mammoth Gold', 'Atlantic Giant', 'Sumo' and 'Prizewinner' (*see also* **Squash**).

Radish, Oriental and winter   Usually large, round or long-pointed roots, which can weigh up to 2kg in the case of Oriental radishes and up to 1kg for winter radishes. Long white Oriental radishes, known as moolis, and coloured-skinned cultivars with red, white or green flesh are included in this category.

Radish, small salad   Quick growing, tender rooted, round to oval with a diameter of approximately 30mm, coloured red, white, occasionally yellow, or red with white lower half. French breakfast types with roots about 75mm long, blunt-ended with white tip of varying proportions. Also white, pointed roots up to 100mm long.

Ray-florets   The outer florets of a flowerhead, such as that of a daisy, often larger than the inner florets.

Rhizome   An underground, usually horizontal, swollen stem containing food reserves, *eg* in bearded irises.

Rhubarb   Although commonly eaten as a dessert this plant is classified as a vegetable for all show purposes.

Root vegetable   For horticultural-show purposes, root vegetables include the following kinds: artichokes (Chinese and Jerusalem), beetroot, carrots, celeriac, kohlrabi, parsnips, potatoes, radishes, salsify, scorzonera, swedes and turnips.

Rose end The end of a potato tuber where the dormant buds, or "eyes", are concentrated.

Salad vegetable A vegetable used in either a raw or cooked state and served in salads as a cold dish. The following examples are kinds that may be used for horticultural-show purposes: beetroot, cabbages, carrots, celeriac, celery, chicory, chives, corn salad or lambs' lettuce, cress, cress (American or land), cucumbers, dandelion (blanched), endive, Florence fennel, kohlrabi, lettuces, mustard or rape, onions (green salad), oriental brassicas, radishes, salad potatoes, sweet peppers, tomatoes, turnips and watercress.

Seedling 1 A young plant that has recently germinated.
2 A plant of any age raised from seed as opposed to one propagated by grafting or other vegetative means.
3 For horticultural-show purposes a distinct new cultivar (variety) raised from seed and not yet named.

Sepal An individual segment of the calyx.

Shrub A woody perennial, often many-stemmed, of smaller structure than a tree and having no distinct bole or trunk.

Soft fruit A fruit having a soft texture and numerous seeds, *eg* a blackberry, currant, gooseberry, loganberry, raspberry or strawberry. Fig and mulberry are not considered soft fruit for show purposes.

Species A group of closely related plants of one genus having the same specific name; *eg Lilium candidum* and *L. martagon* are two species of *Lilium*; *L. martagon* var. *cattaniæ* and *L. martagon* var. *hirsutum* are botanical varieties of one species, *Lilium martagon*.

Spike For horticultural-show purposes, a spike is an unbranched (or only very slightly branched) inflorescence with an elongated axis, bearing either stalked or stalkless flowers, as in a cymbidium, delphinium, foxglove, gladiolus, hollyhock or odontoglossum.

Sport A sport from a particular cultivar (variety) is a plant propagated vegetatively from a mutated part of the parent cultivar (variety).

Spray For horticultural-show purposes, a spray is a branched, many-flowered inflorescence usually on a single main stem.

Squash Fruits of the genus *Cucurbita*. There are two types: summer squash and winter squash. Summer squash are fruit eaten and shown at the immature stage, and include scallops or pattypans, custard marrows and crooknecks – mostly of species *C. pepo*. (Courgettes and marrows could be, but are not, considered in this class.) Winter squash are generally those cultivars whose fruits are eaten at the fully mature stage, and which can be stored for winter use. They are generally of the species *C. maxima* and *C. moschata* but also some *C. pepo*. Cultivars of winter squash include 'Acorn', 'Buttercup', 'Butternut', 'Crown Prince', 'Hubbard's', 'Kabocha', 'Onion Squash', 'Sweet Dumpling', 'Turk's Turban' and 'Vegetable Spaghetti'.

Standard 1 A term that, when applied to a tree or other plant, means a specimen with an upright stem of some length supporting a head, *eg* the standard is a common form for "permanent" orchard trees of apples, pears and plums. Roses, fuchsias, heliotropes and chrysanthemums are ornamental plants readily grown as standards.
2 When applied to a sweet pea or other papilionaceous flowers it describes the, usually upright, back petal of the corolla.
3 When applied to an iris it describes one of the three inner perianth segments.

Stone fruit A fruit with a soft, fleshy interior, surrounding a comparatively large "stone" containing, usually, a solitary seed, *eg* an apricot, cherry, damson, peach or plum.

Strig A term relating to currants and to berries of a similar bearing habit such as jostaberry and worcesterberry. Strig indicates a bunch or, in botanical terms, a complete raceme or panicle of berries. It is best detached from the plant with scissors and should not include any of the woody section at the base.

Succulent A plant with very fleshy leaves or stems or both, *eg* species of *Cotyledon, Crassula, Echeveria, Hoya, Kalanchoe, Sedum, Sempervivum* and most *Cactaceae*.

T-handle This is formed when a fruit or fruits are cut from a vine with a piece of lateral shoot either side of the stalk. This is most commonly found with bunches of grapes so they can be mounted on a stand for exhibition purposes.

Tail The often curved, tapering end of a bean opposite to the stalk.

Tender A tender plant is one that requires a favourable locality or situation and that, under severe climatic conditions, may need some form of protection during winter.
Tree A perennial woody plant with an evident bole or trunk, but sometimes multi-stemmed.
Truss A cluster of flowers or fruits growing from one main stem, as

Glossary

in a pelargonium, polyanthus, rhododendron or tomato.

Tuber A swollen underground stem with buds or "eyes" from which new plants or tubers are produced, *eg* Jerusalem artichoke, tuberous begonia, dahlia, gloriosa, gloxinia, potato and runner bean.

Uniformity The state of being alike in size, shape, condition and colour.

Variety In scientific usage the term "variety" (*varietas*) is a botanical category restricted to a naturally occurring variant of a species; "botanical varieties" are given Latin names, preceded by the abbreviation "var." and begin with a small letter (*eg Paeonia lutea* var. *ludlowii*). Variants of species and hybrids produced by man in cultivation are termed cultivars and are given non-Latin "fancy" names, though some old cultivars, which have had Latin names for many years, retain these names; cultivar names begin with a capital letter and follow directly after the Latin or English name of the species or hybrid concerned, enclosed in single quotation marks (*eg Syringa vulgaris* 'Mont Blanc'; *Dahlia* 'Hamari Sunshine'; potato 'Kestrel'). In English-speaking countries gardeners have long used the word "variety" to cover both "botanical variety" and "cultivar", but as the term "cultivar" is now becoming increasingly accepted, it is recommended that it should be used in show schedules when appropriate.

Vase A vessel for displaying cut flowers in water and having a greater height than the width-measurement of its mouth. Unless otherwise stated in the schedule a vase may contain any number of cultivars (varieties). In floral arrangement classes, vases with one or more than one handle are acceptable. Where standard vases are not provided by show organisers, judges should exercise discretion in regarding as eligible any container that fulfils the function of a vase and conforms to the definition given above, provided that no account is taken of the container when judging the material shown in it.

Vegetable For horticultural-show purposes, a vegetable is a plant (or part of a plant) normally grown in the kitchen garden to be eaten either cooked or less often raw but not usually as dessert or as a pudding. Rhubarb, though commonly eaten as dessert, is classified as a vegetable. Aubergines, beans, courgettes, cucumbers, marrows, mushrooms, okra, peppers, peas, pumpkins, squash, sweet corn and tomatoes, though botanically fruits, are here classified as vegetables.

Veil In leeks, a thin white transparent skin that is present across and above the button where the leaf opens out from the sheath and which is included in the measurements.

INDEX

A

allotments, judging 174, 177–179
alpine, definition 186
alpine strawberries 67, 68, 79, 80, 182
alpine-house plants, judging 132–133
amateurs:
    classification 18
    definition 186
amenity gardens, judging 174–175
American cress 90, 104, 127
"and", use of word 32
annuals:
    classes for 33–35
    definition 186
    judging 131–133
apples 31, 32, 38, 44, 64–65
    classified list 81–86
    cooking 68, 84–85
    dessert 31, 68, 81–830
    dual-purpose 32, 65
apricots 44, 64, 66, 69
arrangements, floral 154
artichokes:
    Chinese 94
    globe 45, 90, 94
    Jerusalem 90, 94
Asian pears 67, 76
asparagus 90, 95
asparagus peas 45, 90, 95
aubergines 45, 95, 176
auriculas 133–135
awards 12–13, 20–23, 35, 150

B

barrel, definition 186
beans 33, 45, 56, 179
    broad 45, 90, 96, 176, 178
    climbing 37, 45, 56, 90, 176
        see also French; runner
    dwarf 37, 45, 56, 90, 176
    dwarf French 45, 90, 176
    French 37, 45, 56, 90
    runner 37, 45, 56, 90, 176
beard, definition 186
beetroot 37, 45, 90, 97, 87, 176
    classes for 33
beginners, encouraging 42
begonias, double tuberous 135
berries 44
Best Bloom 23
Best in Show 23, 55
biennials:
    classes for 34–35
    definition 186
    judging 131
blackberries 66, 69, 177
blackcurrant × gooseberry hybrids 44, 67, 71, 80
blackcurrants 44, 64, 66, 71, 177
blanch, definition 186
blemish, definition 186
bloom:
    best 23
    definitions 186
blueberries 44, 64, 66, 69
bonsai 130, 135
bowl, definition 186
boysenberries 69, 70
bract, definition 186
brassicas, Oriental 47, 92, 98, 115, 176
broad beans 45, 90, 96, 176, 178
broccoli, sprouting 91, 98
Brussels sprouts 45, 91, 99
bulb, definition 186
bulbous plants:
    definition 187
    judging 131
bullaces 66, 70, 72, 85
button, definition 187

C

cabbages 31, 45
    Chinese 91, 99
    green 91, 99
    red 91, 99
    Savoy 91, 99
cacti:
    definition 187
    judging 136
calabrese 46, 91, 100

Index

calamondins 66
calyx, definition 187
cape gooseberries 66, 70
carnations:
    border 137
    perpetual-flowering 137–138
    picotees 137
carrots 46, 176, 178
    classes for 33, 37
    long-pointed 91, 100
    stump-rooted 91, 100
cauliflowers 46, 91
    coloured 101
    white 102
celeriac 91, 102
celery 46, 47, 176
    blanched 103
    green 103
    self-blanching 103
    trench 103
chards 49, 93, 103, 122
cherries 45, 66, 70, 177
chicory 91, 104, 106
chilli peppers 48, 93, 117
Chinese artichokes 94
Chinese cabbages 91, 99
Chinese gooseberries *see* kiwi fruits
chives 91, 104
    see also salad vegetables
choi-sum *see* broccoli
chrysanthemums 38, 130, 138, 143
    specimen plants in pots 142
citrus fruits 44, 66, 71
classes:
    definition 187
    numbering 30
    wording 33–35
collections:
    definition 187
    judging 56
conifers, definition 187
containers:
    definition 187
    judging 182
corm, definition 187
corn salad 91, 104
    see also salad vegetables
corolla, definition 187
corona, definition 187
courgettes 46, 49, 104
cress 91, 104
    see also salad vegetables
    American or land 91, 104
cucumbers 37, 46, 176
    gherkins and pickling types 91, 106
    mini or small 91, 105
    outdoor 91, 105
    under protection 91, 105
cultivar:
    definition 187
    selection 42
    use of word 31
currant × gooseberry hybrids 44, 67, 71, 80
currants 44, 64, 177
    black 66, 71
    other than black 66, 71
cutting fruit or vegetables 56

D

daffodils 143 –147
dahlias 12, 23, 34, 54, 130, 147–152
damsons 66, 72, 85
dandelions 193
    see also salad vegetables
deciduous, definition 187
decisions 61
delphiniums 23, 153
dish:
    constitution 19, 23, 60 –61, 66–67, 90 –93
    definition 187–188
display, definition 188
"dissimilar", avoidance of word 31
"distinct", avoidance of word 31
dual-purpose gardens, judging 174–175

E

endive 91, 106
entries:
    acceptance 60
    avoiding making too many 42
    definition 188
    multiple entry classes 30
    number in class 30, 42
    number per competitor 42, 60
    number per household 60
    recording 22
    time for receipt 28, 29
entry cards 21, 22, 42–43
entry form 29, 39, 42
evergreen, definition 188
everlasting, definition 188
exhibitors 14
    classification 18
    eligibility 60
    suggestions to 41–50
exhibits:
    alteration 61
    constitution 29
    equal merit 35
    from professional gardeners 18
    judging 55
    labelling 22, 42, 60
    naming 22, 60
    not according to schedule (NAS) 55, 61
    number of specimens required 43, 66, 90
    pointing 55
    preparation and presentation 43
    property of exhibitor 60
    uniform treatment 56

F

falls, definition 188
fennel, Florence 46, 91, 106
    see also herbs
figs 45, 64, 66, 72
flags, definition 188
floral arrangements 154
Florence fennel 46, 91, 106
florets, definition 188
flower gardens, judging 176
flower show, how to stage 12–14
flowerhead, definition 188
flowers:
    condition 130
    floating 153 – 154
    judging 130
    preparation and presentation 130
    uniformity 130
foliage 34
    definitions 188
foliage plant:
    definition 188
    judging 38, 163
forced, definition 188
frames, judging 176
French beans 37, 45, 56, 90
fruit gardens, judging 177
fruiting vegetables, miscellaneous 126
fruits:
    "any other" classes 32 – 33, 38, 56
    assessing merit 64
    classification 65
    classified list 81–86
    classified as vegetables 195
    colour 65
    condition 64 – 65
    cutting 56
    definitions 188
    dual-purpose 32, 65
    judging 65–86
    other 32, 38, 56, 80
    points for 66
    preparation and presentation 44–45
    ripeness 32, 64
    size 64–65
    stalks 64
    uniformity 64
fuchsias 155

Index

G

gages 67, 72, 78, 85
gardens:
    inspection 61, 174
    judging 173–179
garlic 46, 92, 107
genus:
    definition 188
    use of word 31
gladioli 23, 130, 156
glasshouses, judging 176
globe artichokes 45, 90, 94
glossary 185–195
gooseberries 32, 64, 66, 72, 176
    blackcurrant × gooseberry
        hybrids 44, 67, 71, 80
gourds:
    edible, definition 188
    ornamental 157
        definition 189
grapes 38, 44 – 45, 64, 177
    glasshouse 66, 73
    outdoor 66, 73
grown in the open, definition 189

H

habit, definition 189
half-hardy, definition 189
handle, definition 189
hanging baskets, judging 182
hardy plants, definition 189
heathers 157
herbaceous perennial,
    definition 189– 190
herbaceous plants:
    definition 190
    judging 131
herbs 92, 108, 177, 178
    definition 189
hilum, definition 190
house plants 162–163
    definition 190
huckleberries 66, 73, 80
hybrid:
    definition 190
    use of word 31

hybrid cane fruits 66, 69

I

inflorescence, definition 190
irises 158

J

Japanese loquats 66, 73, 80
Japanese wineberries 73
Jerusalem artichokes 90, 94
jostaberries 44, 67, 74
judges:
    decisions 61
    duties 21
    non-agreement 55
    numbers 21
    qualifications 21
    suggestions to 53–57
judging:
    clearing show for 22
    engagements 54
    exhibitors' absence during 43
    procedure 54
    speed in 55

K

kales 46, 93, 108
kind:
    definition 190– 191
    use of word 31
kiwanos (horned melons) 67, 74
kiwi fruits 67, 74
kohlrabi 47, 92, 109
kumquats 66

L

labels 21, 22, 42, 57
lambs' lettuce *see* corn salad
leaf mustards 115
leaf vegetables, miscellaneous 126
leeks 46, 176
    blanched 92, 109
    definition 191
    intermediate 92, 109
    pot 92, 110

lettuces 47, 92, 110, 111, 176, 182
liability:
    for injury 13, 61
    for loss 43, 61
loganberries 74
loquats, Japanese 66, 73, 80

M

mangetout 45, 92, 117
marjoram *see* herbs
marrows 12, 37, 47, 92, 111, 176
    definition 191
medlars 32, 64, 67, 74
melons 67, 74, 80
    horned 67, 75
mibuna 115
mint *see* herbs
mizuna 115
mulberries 67, 75
mushrooms 92, 112
"must", use of word 32, 43
mustard 92, 112, 115
    see also salad vegetables

N

narcissi 143–147
NAS *see* not according to schedule
natural, definition 191
nectarines 44, 64, 67, 75, 76, 177
New Zealand spinach 93, 122
not according to schedule 20, 21, 43, 55, 61, 150
    definition 191
novice, definition 191
nuts 67, 75

O

okra 92, 112
onions 18, 33, 47, 176
    250g or under 37, 92, 113
    classes for 33, 37
    green salad 47, 92, 114
    large exhibition 92, 113
    on ropes 92, 114
    pickling 92, 115
"or", use of word 32

orchids 31, 130, 158, 162 – 163
organisation, suggestions on 17–24
Oriental brassicas 47, 92, 115
originality, definition 191
ornamental plants, judging 130–171
ornamental trees and shrubs 132

P

pak choi 115
panicle, definition 191
pansies:
    fancy (exhibition cultivars) 158 – 159
    fancy (garden cultivars) 159
    show 159–160
parsley 48, 115
    see also herbs
parsnips 48, 92, 116, 176
passion fruits 65, 75, 80
peaches 44, 64, 67, 76, 177
pears 32, 39, 45, 64, 65, 177
    Asian 67, 76
    classified list 85
    cooking 67, 76
    dessert 38, 67, 77
peas 45, 48, 92, 116, 176
    asparagus 45, 90, 95
    mangetout 45, 92, 117
    snap 45, 92, 117
pedicel, definition 191
peduncle, definition 191
pelargoniums:
    ivy-leaved 160
    regal 160–161
    zonal 160–161
peppers:
    hot (chilli) 48, 93, 117
    sweet 48, 93, 117
perennials:
    classes 35, 38
    definition 191
perianth, definition 191 –192
persimmons 67, 77, 80
pest infestations 56

Index

petal, definition 192
pineapple guavas 67, 77, 80
pineapples 67, 77
pinks 160
pip, definition 192
plums 38, 45, 65, 177
    classified list 85 – 86
    cooking 67, 78
    dessert 67, 78
points:
    maximum for fruits 56, 66– 67
    maximum for vegetables 56, 90–93
polyanthus 162
pot plants 162–163
    definition 192
potatoes 31, 37, 48, 93, 118, 176
    classes for 33
pots, size 19, 30
primroses 163
Primula species 164
prize cards 21
prizes:
    one per class 61
    point-value 29 – 30
    relative value 29 – 30
    withholding 23, 55,
prizewinners, recording 22
professional gardeners:
    definition 192
    exhibits from 18
protests 19, 21, 23 – 24 , 43, 61
pumpkins 12, 48, 93, 118
    definition 192

Q

quinces 32, 45, 64, 67, 78

R

radishes 48
    Oriental 93, 118
        definition 192
    salad 48, 93, 118
        definition 192
    winter 93, 118
        definition 192

rape 92, 112
    see also salad vegetables
raspberries 38, 67, 79, 177
ray-florets, definition 192
recording entries and prizewinners 22
redcurrants *see* currants, other than black
referees 22 , 61
rhizome, definition 192
rhubarb 48
    definition 192
    forced 93, 119
    natural 93, 119
ripeness of fruit 32, 64
rock-garden plants, judging 132 – 133
root vegetables 127
    definition 193
    miscellaneous 127
rose end, definition 193
roses 13, 54, 130, 164–167, 176
    miniature 167, 168–169
    specimen blooms 167–168
rules 13, 54, 59–61 , 130
    enforcement 28
    stated in schedule 28, 36
runner beans 37, 45, 56, 90, 176

S

sage *see* herbs
salad vegetables 33, 93, 127
    class for 33
    definition 193
salsify 48, 93, 120
savory, summer and winter *see* herbs
Savoy cabbage 91, 99
schedule-makers, suggestions to 27–39
scorzonera 48, 93, 120
seakale 93, 120
seedling, definitions 193
sepal, definition 193
shallots 48
    exhibition 93, 121
    pickling 93, 121

203

"should", use of word 32, 43
show secretary, duties 18–19
shrubs:
    definition 193
    judging 132–133
"similar", avoidance of word 61
size 56, 64, 90
snap peas 45, 92, 117
soft fruit, definition 193
species:
    definition 193
    use of word 31
specimens:
    number required 43, 66, 90
    uniformity 43
spike, definition 193
spinach 49, 93, 122
    New Zealand 93, 122
spinach beet 49, 93, 122
sport, definition 193
spray, definition 193 –194
squashes 49, 93, 122, 123
    definition 194
staging:
    a flower show 12–14, 18–24
    allowing ample time for 42
standard, definition 194
stewards:
    duties 12–14
    suggestions to 19–20
stone fruit, definition 194
strawberries 67, 79, 80, 177
    alpine 67, 68, 79, 80, 182
strig, definition 194
succulents:
    definition 194
    judging 136
swedes 49, 93, 123
sweet corn 49, 93, 123
sweet peas 130, 169
sweet peppers 48, 93, 117
sylvanberries 79

T

T-handle, definition 194
tabling 19
tail, definition 194
tamarillos 67, 79, 80
tarragon *see* herbs
tayberries 79
tender, definition 194 –195
terms, use of 31
thyme *see* herbs
timetable 28, 36
timing of a show 12
tomatoes 37, 49, 93, 124, 125, 176, 182
    classes for 34
tree tomatoes 67, 79, 80
trees:
    definition 195
    judging 132
truss, definition 195
tuber, definition 195
tulips 170–171
turnips 49, 93, 125

U

uniformity:
    definition 195
    importance of 43
utility gardens, judging 174-175

V

variety, definition 195
vase, definition 195
vegetable gardens, judging 176
vegetables:
    "any other" classes 32–33, 37, 56
    assessing merits 90
    colour 90
    condition 90
    cutting 56
    definition 195 –196
    fruit classified as 195
    judging 90-127
    maximum points for 56, 90–93
    preparation and presentation 45–49
    single specimens, judging 56
    size 56

uniformity 56
veil, definition 196
venue for a show 12
violas 130, 171

W

watercress 93, 182
   see also salad vegetables
whitecurrants *see* currants,
   other than black
windowboxes, judging 176
worcesterberries 44, 67, 80